BEOWULF

SPARK PUBLISHING

© 2003, 2007 by Spark Publishing, A Division of Barnes & Noble

This Spark Publishing edition 2014 by SparkNotes LLC, an Affiliate of Barnes & Noble

122 Fifth Avenue
New York, NY 10011
www.sparknotes.com

ISBN 978-1-4114-6944-0

Please submit changes or report errors to www.sparknotes.com/errors.

Printed in Canada

10 9 8 7 6 5 4 3 2 1

CONTENTS

CONTEXT

THOUGH IT IS OFTEN VIEWED both as the archetypal Anglo-Saxon literary work and as a cornerstone of modern literature, *Beowulf* has a peculiar history that complicates both its historical and its canonical position in English literature. By the time the story of *Beowulf* was composed by an unknown Anglo-Saxon poet around 700 A.D., much of its material had been in circulation in oral narrative for many years. The Anglo-Saxon and Scandinavian peoples had invaded the island of Britain and settled there several hundred years earlier, bringing with them several closely related Germanic languages that would evolve into Old English. Elements of the *Beowulf* story—including its setting and characters—date back to the period before the migration. The action of the poem takes place around 500 A.D. Many of the characters in the poem—the Swedish and Danish royal family members, for example—correspond to actual historical figures. Originally pagan warriors, the Anglo-Saxon and Scandinavian invaders experienced a large-scale conversion to Christianity at the end of the sixth century. Though still an old pagan story, *Beowulf* thus came to be told by a Christian poet. The *Beowulf* poet is often at pains to attribute Christian thoughts and motives to his characters, who frequently behave in distinctly un-Christian ways. The *Beowulf* that we read today is therefore probably quite unlike the *Beowulf* with which the first Anglo-Saxon audiences were familiar. The element of religious tension is quite common in Christian Anglo-Saxon writings (*The Dream of the Rood,* for example), but the combination of a pagan story with a Christian narrator is fairly unusual. The plot of the poem concerns Scandinavian culture, but much of the poem's narrative intervention reveals that the poet's culture was somewhat different from that of his ancestors, and that of his characters as well.

The world that *Beowulf* depicts and the heroic code of honor that defines much of the story is a relic of pre–Anglo-Saxon culture. The story is set in Scandinavia, before the migration. Though it is a traditional story—part of a Germanic oral tradition—the poem as we have it is thought to be the work of a single poet. It was composed in England (not in Scandinavia) and is historical in its perspective, recording the values and culture of a bygone era. Many of those values, including the heroic code, were still operative to some degree in when the poem was written. These values had evolved to some extent in the intervening centuries and were continuing to change. In the Scandinavian world of the story, tiny tribes of people rally around strong kings, who protect their people from danger—especially from confrontations with other tribes. The warrior culture that results from this early feudal arrangement is extremely important, both to the story and to our understanding of Saxon civilization. Strong kings demand bravery and loyalty from their warriors, whom they repay with treasures won in war. Mead-halls such as Heorot in *Beowulf* were places where warriors would gather in the presence of their lord to drink, boast, tell stories, and receive gifts. Although these mead-halls offered sanctuary, the early Middle Ages were a dangerous time, and the paranoid sense of foreboding and doom that runs throughout *Beowulf* evidences the constant fear of invasion that plagued Scandinavian society.

Only a single manuscript of *Beowulf* survived the Anglo-Saxon era. For many centuries, the manuscript was all but forgotten, and, in the 1700s, it was nearly destroyed in a fire. It was not until the nineteenth century that widespread interest in the document emerged among scholars and translators of Old English. For the first hundred years of *Beowulf*'s prominence, interest in the poem was primarily historical—the text was viewed as a source of information about the Anglo-Saxon era. It was not until 1936, when the Oxford scholar J. R. R. Tolkien (who later wrote *The Hobbit* and *The Lord of the Rings,* works heavily influenced by *Beowulf*) published a groundbreaking paper entitled "*Beowulf:* The Monsters and the Critics" that the manuscript gained recognition as a serious work of art.

Beowulf is now widely taught and is often presented as the first important work of English literature, creating the impression that *Beowulf* is in some way the source of the English canon. But because it was not widely read until the 1800s and not widely regarded as an important artwork until the 1900s, *Beowulf* has had little direct impact on the development of English poetry. In fact, Chaucer, Shakespeare, Marlowe, Pope, Shelley, Keats, and most other important English writers before the 1930s had little or no knowledge of the epic. It was not until the mid-to-late twentieth century that *Beowulf* began to influence writers, and, since then, it has had a marked impact on the work of many important novelists and poets, including W. H. Auden, Geoffrey Hill, Ted Hughes, and Seamus Heaney, the 1995 recipient of the Nobel Prize in Literature, whose recent translation of the epic is the edition used for this SparkNote.

Old English Poetry

Beowulf is often referred to as the first important work of literature in English, even though it was written in Old English, an ancient form of the language that slowly evolved into the English now spoken. Compared to modern English, Old English is heavily Germanic, with little influence from Latin or French. As English history developed, after the French Normans conquered the Anglo-Saxons in 1066, Old English was gradually broadened by offerings from those languages. Thus modern English is derived from a number of sources. As a result, its vocabulary is rich with synonyms. The word *kingly*, for instance, descends from the Anglo-Saxon word *cyning*, meaning "king," while the synonym *royal* comes from a French word and the synonym *regal* from a Latin word.

Fortunately, most students encountering *Beowulf* read it in a form translated into modern English. Still, a familiarity with the rudiments of Anglo-Saxon poetry enables a deeper understanding of the *Beowulf* text. Old English poetry is highly formal, but its form is quite unlike anything in modern English. Each line of Old English poetry is divided into two halves, separated by a caesura, or pause, and is often represented by a gap on the page, as the following example demonstrates:

Setton him to heafdon   hilde-randas....

Because Anglo-Saxon poetry existed in oral tradition long before it was written down, the verse form contains complicated rules for alliteration designed to help scops, or poets, remember the many thousands of lines they were required to know by heart. Each of the two halves of an Anglo-Saxon line contains two stressed syllables, and an alliterative pattern *must* be carried over across the caesura. Any of the stressed syllables may alliterate *except* the last syllable; so the first and second syllables may alliterate with the third together, or the first and third may alliterate alone, or the second and third may alliterate alone. For instance:

Lade ne letton.   Leoht eastan com.

Lade, letton, leoht, and *eastan* are the four stressed words.

In addition to these rules, Old English poetry often features a distinctive set of rhetorical devices. The most common of these is the *kenning*, used throughout *Beowulf*. A kenning is a short metaphorical description of a thing used in place of the thing's name; thus a ship might be called a "sea-rider," or a king a "ring-giver." Some translations employ kennings almost as frequently as they appear in the original. Others moderate the use of kennings in deference to a modern sensibility. But the Old English version of the epic is full of them, and they are perhaps the most important rhetorical device present in Old English poetry.

PLOT OVERVIEW

KING HROTHGAR OF DENMARK, a descendant of the great king Shield Sheafson, enjoys a prosperous and successful reign. He builds a great mead-hall, called Heorot, where his warriors can gather to drink, receive gifts from their lord, and listen to stories sung by the scops, or bards. But the jubilant noise from Heorot angers Grendel, a horrible demon who lives in the swamplands of Hrothgar's kingdom. Grendel terrorizes the Danes every night, killing them and defeating their efforts to fight back. The Danes suffer many years of fear, danger, and death at the hands of Grendel. Eventually, however, a young Geatish warrior named Beowulf hears of Hrothgar's plight. Inspired by the challenge, Beowulf sails to Denmark with a small company of men, determined to defeat Grendel.

Hrothgar, who had once done a great favor for Beowulf's father Ecgtheow, accepts Beowulf's offer to fight Grendel and holds a feast in the hero's honor. During the feast, an envious Dane named Unferth taunts Beowulf and accuses him of being unworthy of his reputation. Beowulf responds with a boastful description of some of his past accomplishments. His confidence cheers the Danish warriors, and the feast lasts merrily into the night. At last, however, Grendel arrives. Beowulf fights him unarmed, proving himself stronger than the demon, who is terrified. As Grendel struggles to escape, Beowulf tears the monster's arm off. Mortally wounded, Grendel slinks back into the swamp to die. The severed arm is hung high in the mead-hall as a trophy of victory.

Overjoyed, Hrothgar showers Beowulf with gifts and treasure at a feast in his honor. Songs are sung in praise of Beowulf, and the celebration lasts late into the night. But another threat is approaching. Grendel's mother, a swamp-hag who lives in a desolate lake, comes to Heorot seeking revenge for her son's death. She murders Aeschere, one of Hrothgar's most trusted advisers, before slinking away. To avenge Aeschere's death, the company travels to the murky swamp, where Beowulf dives into the water and fights Grendel's mother in her underwater lair. He kills her with a sword forged for a giant, then, finding Grendel's corpse, decapitates it and brings the head as a prize to Hrothgar. The Danish countryside is now purged of its treacherous monsters.

The Danes are again overjoyed, and Beowulf's fame spreads across the kingdom. Beowulf departs after a sorrowful goodbye to Hrothgar, who has treated him like a son. He returns to Geatland, where he and his men are reunited with their king and queen, Hygelac and Hygd, to whom Beowulf recounts his adventures in Denmark. Beowulf then hands over most of his treasure to Hygelac, who, in turn, rewards him.

In time, Hygelac is killed in a war against the Shylfings, and, after Hygelac's son dies, Beowulf ascends to the throne of the Geats. He rules wisely for fifty years, bringing prosperity to Geatland. When Beowulf is an old man, however, a thief disturbs a barrow, or mound, where a great dragon lies guarding a horde of treasure. Enraged, the dragon emerges from the barrow and begins unleashing fiery destruction upon the Geats. Sensing his own death approaching, Beowulf goes to fight the dragon. With the aid of Wiglaf, he succeeds in killing the beast, but at a heavy cost. The dragon bites Beowulf in the neck, and its fiery venom kills him moments after their encounter. The Geats fear that their enemies will attack them now that Beowulf is dead. According to Beowulf's wishes, they burn their departed king's body on a huge funeral pyre and then bury him with a massive treasure in a barrow overlooking the sea.

CHARACTER LIST

PRINCIPAL CHARACTERS

Beowulf   The protagonist of the epic, Beowulf is a Geatish hero who fights the monster Grendel, Grendel's mother, and a fire-breathing dragon. Beowulf's boasts and encounters reveal him to be the strongest, ablest warrior around. In his youth, he personifies all of the best values of the heroic culture. In his old age, he proves a wise and effective ruler.

King Hrothgar   The king of the Danes. Hrothgar enjoys military success and prosperity until Grendel terrorizes his realm. A wise and aged ruler, Hrothgar represents a different kind of leadership from that exhibited by the youthful warrior Beowulf. He is a father figure to Beowulf and a model for the kind of king that Beowulf becomes.

Grendel   A demon descended from Cain, Grendel preys on Hrothgar's warriors in the king's mead-hall, Heorot. Because his ruthless and miserable existence is part of the retribution exacted by God for Cain's murder of Abel, Grendel fits solidly within the ethos of vengeance that governs the world of the poem.

Grendel's mother   An unnamed swamp-hag, Grendel's mother seems to possess fewer human qualities than Grendel, although her terrorization of Heorot is explained by her desire for vengeance—a human motivation.

The dragon   An ancient, powerful serpent, the dragon guards a horde of treasure in a hidden mound. Beowulf's fight with the dragon constitutes the third and final part of the epic.

OTHER DANES

Shield Sheafson The legendary Danish king from whom Hrothgar is descended, Shield Sheafson is the mythical founder who inaugurates a long line of Danish rulers and embodies the Danish tribe's highest values of heroism and leadership. The poem opens with a brief account of his rise from orphan to warrior-king, concluding, "That was one good king" (11).

Beow The second king listed in the genealogy of Danish rulers with which the poem begins. Beow is the son of Shield Sheafson and father of Halfdane. The narrator presents Beow as a gift from God to a people in need of a leader. He exemplifies the maxim, "Behavior that's admired / is the path to power among people everywhere" (24–25).

Halfdane The father of Hrothgar, Heorogar, Halga, and an unnamed daughter who married a king of the Swedes, Halfdane succeeded Beow as ruler of the Danes.

Wealhtheow Hrothgar's wife, the gracious queen of the Danes.

Unferth A Danish warrior who is jealous of Beowulf, Unferth is unable or unwilling to fight Grendel, thus proving himself inferior to Beowulf.

Hrethric Hrothgar's elder son, Hrethric stands to inherit the Danish throne, but Hrethric's older cousin Hrothulf will prevent him from doing so. Beowulf offers to support the youngster's prospect of becoming king by hosting him in Geatland and giving him guidance.

Hrothmund The second son of Hrothgar.

Hrothulf Hrothgar's nephew, Hrothulf betrays and usurps his cousin, Hrethic, the rightful heir to the Danish throne. Hrothulf's treachery contrasts with Beowulf's loyalty to Hygelac in helping his son to the throne.

Aeschere   Hrothgar's trusted adviser.

OTHER GEATS

Hygelac   Beowulf's uncle, king of the Geats, and husband of Hygd. Hygelac heartily welcomes Beowulf back from Denmark.

Hygd   Hygelac's wife, the young, beautiful, and intelligent queen of the Geats. Hygd is contrasted with Queen Modthryth.

Wiglaf   A young kinsman and retainer of Beowulf who helps him in the fight against the dragon while all of the other warriors run away. Wiglaf adheres to the heroic code better than Beowulf's other retainers, thereby proving himself a suitable successor to Beowulf.

Ecgtheow   Beowulf's father, Hygelac's brother-in-law, and Hrothgar's friend. Ecgtheow is dead by the time the story begins, but he lives on through the noble reputation that he made for himself during his life and in his dutiful son's remembrances.

King Hrethel   The Geatish king who took Beowulf in as a ward after the death of Ecgtheow, Beowulf's father.

Breca   Beowulf's childhood friend, whom he defeated in a swimming match. Unferth alludes to the story of their contest, and Beowulf then relates it in detail.

OTHER FIGURES MENTIONED

Sigemund   A figure from Norse mythology, famous for slaying a dragon. Sigemund's story is told in praise of Beowulf and foreshadows Beowulf's encounter with the dragon.

King Heremod An evil king of legend. The scop, or bard, at Heorot discusses King Heremod as a figure who contrasts greatly with Beowulf.

Queen Modthryth A wicked queen of legend who punishes anyone who looks at her the wrong way. Modthryth's story is told in order to contrast her cruelty with Hygd's gentle and reasonable behavior.

Analysis of Major
Characters

Beowulf

Beowulf exemplifies the traits of the perfect hero. The poem explores his heroism in two separate phases—youth and age—and through three separate and increasingly difficult conflicts—with Grendel, Grendel's mother, and the dragon. Although we can view these three encounters as expressions of the heroic code, there is perhaps a clearer division between Beowulf's youthful heroism as an unfettered warrior and his mature heroism as a reliable king. These two phases of his life, separated by fifty years, correspond to two different models of virtue, and much of the moral reflection in the story centers on differentiating these two models and on showing how Beowulf makes the transition from one to the other.

In his youth, Beowulf is a great warrior, characterized predominantly by his feats of strength and courage, including his fabled swimming match against Breca. He also perfectly embodies the manners and values dictated by the Germanic heroic code, including loyalty, courtesy, and pride. His defeat of Grendel and Grendel's mother validates his reputation for bravery and establishes him fully as a hero. In first part of the poem, Beowulf matures little, as he possesses heroic qualities in abundance from the start. Having purged Denmark of its plagues and established himself as a hero, however, he is ready to enter into a new phase of his life. Hrothgar, who becomes a mentor and father figure to the young warrior, begins to deliver advice about how to act as a wise ruler. Though Beowulf does not become king for many years, his exemplary career as a warrior has served in part to prepare him for his ascension to the throne.

The second part of the story, set in Geatland, skips over the middle of Beowulf's career and focuses on the very end of his life. Through a series of retrospectives, however, we recover much of what happens during this gap and therefore are able to see how Beowulf comports himself as both a warrior and a king. The period following Hygelac's death is an important transitional moment for Beowulf. Instead of rushing for the throne himself, as Hrothulf does in Denmark, he supports Hygelac's son, the rightful heir. With this gesture of loyalty and respect for the throne, he proves himself worthy of kingship.

In the final episode—the encounter with the dragon—the poet reflects further on how the responsibilities of a king, who must act for the good of the people and not just for his own glory, differ from those of the heroic warrior. In light of these meditations, Beowulf's moral status becomes somewhat ambiguous at the poem's end. Though he is deservedly celebrated as a great hero and leader, his last courageous fight is also somewhat rash. The poem suggests that, by sacrificing himself, Beowulf unnecessarily leaves his people without a king, exposing them to danger from other tribes. To understand Beowulf's death strictly as a personal failure, however, is to neglect the overwhelming emphasis given to fate in this last portion of the poem. The conflict with the dragon has an aura of inevitability about it. Rather than a conscious choice, the battle can also be interpreted as a matter in which Beowulf has very little choice or free will at all. Additionally, it is hard to blame him for acting according to the dictates of his warrior culture.

GRENDEL

Likely the poem's most memorable creation, Grendel is one of the three monsters that Beowulf battles. His nature is ambiguous. Though he has many animal attributes and a grotesque, monstrous appearance, he seems to be guided by vaguely human emotions and impulses, and he shows more of an interior life than one might expect. Exiled to the swamplands outside the boundaries of human society, Grendel is an outcast who seems to long to be reinstated. The poet hints that behind Grendel's aggression against the Danes lies loneliness and jealousy. By lineage, Grendel is a member of "Cain's clan, whom the creator had outlawed / and condemned as outcasts." (106–107). He is thus descended from a figure who epitomizes resentment and malice. While the poet somewhat sympathetically suggests that Grendel's deep bitterness about being excluded from the revelry in the mead-hall owes, in part, to his accursed status, he also points out that Grendel is "[m]alignant by nature" and that he has "never show[n] remorse" (137).

HROTHGAR

Hrothgar, the aged ruler of the Danes who accepts Beowulf's help in the first part of the story, aids Beowulf's development into maturity. Hrothgar is a relatively static character, a force of stability in the social realm. Although he is as solidly rooted in the heroic code as Beowulf is, his old age and his experience with both good and ill fortune have caused him to develop a more reflective attitude toward heroism than Beowulf possesses. He is aware of both the privileges and the dangers of power, and he warns his young protégé not to give in to pride and always to remember that blessings may turn to grief. Hrothgar's meditations on heroism and leadership, which take into account a hero's entire life span rather than just his valiant youth, reveal the contrast between youth and old age that forms the turning point in Beowulf's own development.

UNFERTH

Unferth's challenge to Beowulf's honor differentiates him from Beowulf and helps to reveal some of the subtleties of the heroic code that the warriors must follow. Unferth is presented as a lesser man, a foil for the near-perfect Beowulf. (A foil is a character whose traits contrast with and thereby accentuate those of another character.) The bitterness of Unferth's chiding of Beowulf about his swimming match with Breca clearly reflects his jealousy of the attention that Beowulf receives. It probably also stems from his shame at being unable to protect Heorot himself—he is clearly not the sort of great warrior whom legend will remember. While boasting is a proper and acceptable form of self-assertion, Unferth's harsh words show that it ought not to be bitter or disparaging of others. Rather than heroism, Unferth's blustering reveals pride and resentment. Later, Unferth's gift of his sword for Beowulf's fight against Grendel's mother heals Unferth's breach of hospitality, but it does little to improve his heroic status. Unlike Beowulf, Unferth is clearly afraid to fight the monster himself.

WIGLAF

Wiglaf, one of Beowulf's kinsmen and thanes, is the only warrior brave enough to help the hero in his fight against the dragon. Wiglaf conforms perfectly to the heroic code in that he is willing to die attempting to defeat the opponent and, more importantly, to save his lord. In this regard, Wiglaf appears as a reflection of the young Beowulf in the first part of the story—a warrior who is strong, fearless, valiant, and loyal. He embodies Beowulf's statement from the early scenes of the poem that it is always better to act than to grieve. Wiglaf thus represents the next generation of heroism and the future of the kingdom. His bravery and solid bearing provide the single glint of optimism in the final part of the story, which, for the most part, is dominated by a tone of despair at what the future holds.

THEMES, MOTIFS & SYMBOLS

THEMES

Themes are the fundamental and often universal ideas explored in a literary work.

THE IMPORTANCE OF ESTABLISHING IDENTITY

As Beowulf is essentially a record of heroic deeds, the concept of identity—of which the two principal components are ancestral heritage and individual reputation—is clearly central to the poem. The opening passages introduce the reader to a world in which every male figure is known as his father's son. Characters in the poem are unable to talk about their identity or even introduce themselves without referring to family lineage. This concern with family history is so prominent because of the poem's emphasis on kinship bonds. Characters take pride in ancestors who have acted valiantly, and they attempt to live up to the same standards as those ancestors.

While heritage may provide models for behavior and help to establish identity—as with the line of Danish kings discussed early on—a good reputation is the key to solidifying and augmenting one's identity. For example, Shield Sheafson, the legendary originator of the Danish royal line, was orphaned; because he was in a sense fatherless, valiant deeds were the only means by which he could construct an identity for himself. While Beowulf's pagan warrior culture seems not to have a concept of the afterlife, it sees fame as a way of ensuring that an individual's memory will continue on after death—an understandable preoccupation in a world where death seems always to be knocking at the door.

TENSIONS BETWEEN THE HEROIC CODE AND OTHER VALUE SYSTEMS

Much of Beowulf is devoted to articulating and illustrating the Germanic heroic code, which values strength, courage, and loyalty in warriors; hospitality, generosity, and political skill in kings; ceremoniousness in women; and good reputation in all people. Traditional and much respected, this code is vital to warrior societies as a means of understanding their relationships to the world and the menaces lurking beyond their boundaries. All of the characters' moral judgments stem from the code's mandates. Thus individual actions can be seen only as either conforming to or violating the code.

The poem highlights the code's points of tension by recounting situations that expose its internal contradictions in values. The poem contains several stories that concern divided loyalties, situations for which the code offers no practical guidance about how to act. For example, the poet relates that the Danish Hildeburh marries the Frisian king. When, in the war between the Danes and the Frisians, both her Danish brother and her Frisian son are killed, Hildeburh is left doubly grieved. The code is also often in tension with the values of medieval Christianity. While the code maintains that honor is gained during life through deeds, Christianity asserts that glory lies in the afterlife. Similarly, while the warrior culture dictates that it is always better to retaliate than to mourn, Christian doctrine advocates a peaceful, forgiving attitude toward one's enemies. Throughout the poem, the poet strains to accommodate these two sets of values. Though he is Christian, he cannot (and does not seem to want to) deny the fundamental pagan values of the story.

THE DIFFERENCE BETWEEN A GOOD WARRIOR AND A GOOD KING

Over the course of the poem, Beowulf matures from a valiant combatant into a wise leader. His transition demonstrates that a differing set of values accompanies each of his two roles. The difference between these two sets of values manifests itself early on in the outlooks of Beowulf and King Hrothgar. Whereas the youthful Beowulf, having nothing to lose, desires personal glory, the aged Hrothgar, having much to lose, seeks protection for his people. Though these two outlooks are somewhat oppositional, each character acts as society dictates he should given his particular role in society.

While the values of the warrior become clear through Beowulf's example throughout the poem, only in the poem's more didactic moments are the responsibilities of a king to his people discussed. The heroic code requires that a king reward the loyal service of his warriors with gifts and praise. It also holds that he must provide them with protection and the sanctuary of a lavish mead-hall. Hrothgar's speeches, in particular, emphasize the value of creating stability in a precarious and chaotic world. He also speaks at length about the king's role in diplomacy, both with his own warriors and with other tribes.

Beowulf's own tenure as king elaborates on many of the same points. His transition from warrior to king, and, in particular, his final battle with the dragon, rehash the dichotomy between the duties of a heroic warrior and those of a heroic king. In the eyes of several of the Geats, Beowulf's bold encounter with the dragon is morally ambiguous because it dooms them to a kingless state in which they remain vulnerable to attack by their enemies. Yet Beowulf also demonstrates the sort of restraint proper to kings when, earlier in his life, he refrains from usurping Hygelac's throne, choosing instead to uphold the line of succession by supporting the appointment of Hygelac's son. But since all of these pagan kings were great warriors in their youth, the tension between these two important roles seems inevitable and ultimately irreconcilable.

MOTIFS

Motifs are recurring structures, contrasts, and literary devices that can help to develop and inform the text's major themes.

MONSTERS

In Christian medieval culture, *monster* was the word that referred to birth defects, which were always understood as an ominous sign from God—a sign of transgression or of bad things to come. In keeping with this idea, the monsters that Beowulf must fight in this Old English poem shape the poem's plot and seem to represent an inhuman or alien presence in society that must be exorcised for the society's safety. They are all outsiders, existing beyond the boundaries of human realms. Grendel's and his mother's encroachment upon human society—they wreak havoc in Heorot—forces Beowulf to kill the two beasts for order to be restored.

To many readers, the three monsters that Beowulf slays all seem to have a symbolic or allegorical meaning. For instance, since Grendel is descended from the biblical figure Cain, who slew his own brother, Grendel often has been understood to represent the evil in Scandinavian society of marauding and killing others. A traditional figure of medieval folklore and a common Christian symbol of sin, the dragon may represent an external malice that must be conquered to prove a hero's goodness. Because Beowulf's encounter with the dragon ends in mutual destruction, the dragon may also be interpreted as a symbolic representation of the inevitable encounter with death itself.

The Oral Tradition

Intimately connected to the theme of the importance of establishing one's identity is the oral tradition, which preserves the lessons and lineages of the past, and helps to spread reputations. Indeed, in a culture that has little interaction with writing, only the spoken word can allow individuals to learn about others and make their own stories known. This emphasis on oral communication explains the prevalence of bards' tales (such as the Heorot scop's relating of the Finnsburg episode) and warriors' boastings (such as Beowulf's telling of the Breca story). From a broader perspective, Beowulf itself contributes to the tradition of oral celebration of cultural heroes. Like Homer's *Iliad* and *Odyssey*, Beowulf was passed on orally over many generations before being written down.

The Mead-Hall

The poem contains two examples of mead-halls: Hrothgar's great hall of Heorot, in Denmark, and Hygelac's hall in Geatland. Both function as important cultural institutions that provide light and warmth, food and drink, and singing and revelry. Historically, the mead-hall represented a safe haven for warriors returning from battle, a small zone of refuge within a dangerous and precarious external world that continuously offered the threat of attack by neighboring peoples. The mead-hall was also a place of community, where traditions were preserved, loyalty was rewarded, and, perhaps most important, stories were told and reputations were spread.

SYMBOLS

Symbols are objects, characters, figures, and colors used to represent abstract ideas or concepts. Because ritual behaviors and tokens of loyalty are so central to pagan Germanic culture, most of the objects mentioned in Beowulf have symbolic status not just for the readers but also for the characters in the poem.

The Golden Torque

The collar or necklace that Wealhtheow gives Beowulf is a symbol of the bond of loyalty between her people and Beowulf—and, by extension, the Geats. Its status as a symbolic object is renewed when we learn that Hygelac died in battle wearing it, furthering the ideas of kinship and continuity.

The Banquet

The great banquet at Heorot after the defeat of Grendel represents the restoration of order and harmony to the Danish people. The preparation involves the rebuilding of the damaged mead-hall, which, in conjunction with the banquet itself, symbolizes the rebirth of the community. The speeches and giving of gifts, essential components of this society's interactions, contribute as well to the sense of wholeness renewed.

SYMBOLS

SUMMARY & ANALYSIS

LINES 1-300

SUMMARY

So. The Spear-Danes in days gone by
and the kings who ruled them had courage and greatness.
(See QUOTATIONS, *p. 49)*

The narrator opens the poem with a discussion of Shield Sheafson, a great king of the ancient Danes and the founder of their royal line. He began life as a foundling (an infant abandoned by his parents) but quickly rose to be strong and powerful. All of the clans had to pay him tribute, and, when he died, he was honored with an elaborate funeral ceremony. His body was put into a boat, covered with treasures and armor, and cast off to sea. Shield Sheafson's life ended as it began, with him cast adrift on the water.

Sheafson's son, the renowned Beow, inherited the kingdom after his father's death. In time, Beow too passed away and Halfdane, his son, became king. After Halfdane, Hrothgar stepped forward to rule the Danes. Under Hrothgar, the kingdom prospered and enjoyed great military success, and Hrothgar decided to construct a monument to his success—a mead-hall where he would distribute booty to his retainers. The hall was called Heorot, and there the men gathered with their lord to drink mead, a beerlike beverage, and listen to the songs of the bards.

For a time, the kingdom enjoyed peace and prosperity. But, one night, Grendel, a demon descended from Cain (who, according to the Bible, slew his brother Abel), emerged from the swampy lowlands, to listen to the nightly entertainment at Heorot. The bards' songs about God's creation of the earth angered the monster. Once the men in the mead-hall fell asleep, Grendel lumbered inside and slaughtered thirty men. Hrothgar's warriors were powerless against him.

The following night, Grendel struck again, and he has continued to wreak havoc on the Danes for twelve years. He has taken over Heorot, and Hrothgar and his men remain unable to challenge him. They make offerings at pagan shrines in hopes of harming Grendel, but their efforts are fruitless. The Danes endure constant terror, and their suffering is so extreme that the news of it travels far and wide.

At this time, Beowulf, nephew of the Geatish king Hygelac, is the greatest hero in the world. He lives in Geatland, a realm not far from Denmark, in what is now southern Sweden. When Beowulf hears tales of the destruction wrought by Grendel, he decides to travel to the land of the Danes and help Hrothgar defeat the demon. He voyages across the sea with fourteen of his bravest warriors until he reaches Hrothgar's kingdom.

Seeing that the newcomers are dressed in armor and carrying shields and other equipment for combat, the watchman who guards the Danish coast stops Beowulf and his crew and demands to know their business. He admits that he has never seen outsiders come ashore so fearlessly and guesses that Beowulf is a noble hero. Beowulf explains that he is the son of Ecgtheow and owes his loyalty to Hygelac. He says that he has heard about the monster wreaking havoc on the Danes and has come to help Hrothgar. The watchman gives his consent and tells Beowulf that he believes his story. He tells the Geats to follow him, mentioning that he will order one of the Danes to watch Beowulf's ship for him.

ANALYSIS

Behaviour that's admired
is the path to power among people everywhere.

(See QUOTATIONS, *p. 51)*

It is not surprising that *Beowulf* begins with a tribute to the ancestry of King Hrothgar, since within the warrior culture that the poem depicts, patriarchal lineage is an extremely important component of one's identity. Characters are regularly named as the sons of their fathers—Beowulf, for example, is often referred to as "Ecgtheow's son." Patriarchal history anchors the story in a linear time frame that stretches forward and backward through the generations. In light of the great importance of familial lineage in this culture, it is interesting that Shield Sheafson, who inaugurates the Danish royal line, is an orphan—he is both founder and "foundling." The reader has the sense that if this ordinary personage had not been fatherless, of unknown lineage, the story could have no definitive starting point. We later learn that Beowulf was also left fatherless at a young age.

The delineation of a heroic code is one of the most important preoccupations of the poem. In this first section, some of the central tenets of this code become apparent. In the story of Sheafson in the poem's opening lines, the poet offers a sketch of the life of a successful hero. Sheafson's greatness is measured by the number of clans that he conquers. As the defeated have to pay him tribute, it is clear that strength leads to the acquisition of treasure and gold. In the world of the poem, warriors are bound to their lords by ties of deep loyalty, which the lords maintain through their protection of their warriors and also through ritualized gestures of generosity, or gift-giving. Because their king is powerful, Sheafson's warriors receive treasure. A hero is therefore defined, in part, by his ability to help his community by performing heroic deeds and by doling out heroic sums of treasure. Because Sheafson receives so much booty from his conquests, the poet says of him, "That was one good king" (11) Hrothgar is likewise presented as a good leader, because he erects the mead-hall Heorot for his men.

Another major aspect of the heroic code in *Beowulf* is eloquence in speech. Beowulf is imposing not only because of his physical presence but also because of his powerful oratorical skill. Speech and poetry were extremely important among the Anglo-Saxons and Scandinavians, as they often are in civilizations that rely on oral narratives to preserve history and myth (characters in Homer's *Iliad* are also judged by how they speak). Beowulf's boastful demeanor as he declares his intention to slay the monster is not an indication of undue vanity but rather a customary part of heroic behavior. The watchman's reply that

> [a]nyone with gumption
> and a sharp mind will take the measure
> of two things: what's said and what's done

follows logically from Beowulf's value of eloquence. In the watchman's eyes, brave words must be backed up by brave deeds (287–289).

A well-won reputation ensures that a warrior will become a part of history, of the social fabric of his culture, as the inclusion of the story of Sheafson in the poem immediately reminds us. Throughout the epic, fame is presented as a bulwark against the oblivion of death, which lurks everywhere in the poem and casts a sobering pall over even the most shining acts of heroism. The description of Sheafson's funeral foreshadows the poem's final scene, which depicts the funeral of another heroic king. The tales of heroism that unfold in the intervening lines are thus framed, like life itself, within the envelope of death. The sea acts as another important and ever-present boundary in *Beowulf*; the sea-burial with which the poem begins helps to establish the inexorable margins of life in the story.

LINES 301-709

SUMMARY

The watchman guides Beowulf and his men from the coast to the mead-hall, Heorot, where he takes his leave. A herald named Wulfgar, who is renowned for his wisdom, stops Beowulf and asks him to state his business with Hrothgar. Beowulf introduces himself and requests to speak to the king. Wulfgar, impressed with the group's appearance and bearing, takes Beowulf's message immediately to Hrothgar. Hrothgar tells Wulfgar that he remembers Beowulf from when he was a young boy and recalls his friendship with Beowulf's father, Ecgtheow. He says that he has heard tales of Beowulf's great prowess—one story holds that the Geat has the strength of thirty men in each of his hands—and hopes that Beowulf has come to help the Danes against Grendel. He orders Wulfgar to welcome the Geats to Denmark.

Beowulf comes before Hrothgar, whom he greets solemnly. Beowulf recounts some of his past glories and offers to fight Grendel unarmed. Hrothgar recounts a feud during which Beowulf's father killed Heatholaf, a member of the Wulfing tribe. Hrothgar sent treasure to the Wulfings to mend the feud, and Beowulf's father pledged his allegiance to Hrothgar. Hrothgar then accepts Beowulf's offer to fight Grendel, though he warns him that many heroes have died in the mead-hall trying to battle the monster. He invites the Geats to sit and enjoy a feast in Heorot with the Danish warriors.

At the feast, a Dane named Unferth, envious of his kinsmen's admiration of Beowulf, begins to taunt the Geat. He claims that Beowulf once lost a swimming match against Breca and that Beowulf will meet with defeat for a second time when he faces Grendel in the mead-hall. Unruffled, Beowulf accuses Unferth of drunkenness and describes his own version of what happened in the swimming match. Carrying swords to defend themselves against sea monsters, he and Breca had struggled in icy waters for five days and five nights when suddenly Beowulf found himself pulled under by a monster. After slaying the monster and eight other sea beasts, Beowulf was washed ashore on the coast of Finland. Beowulf notes that neither

Unferth nor Breca could have survived such an adventure and mocks Unferth by pointing out his obvious helplessness against Grendel.

Beowulf's confidence cheers the whole hall, and soon the warriors are laughing and drinking happily. Wealhtheow, wife of Hrothgar and queen of the Danes, enters with the ceremonial goblet, which she offers to everyone in the room. She thanks God for sending Beowulf to fight Grendel, and Beowulf replies with a formal boast, stating that he will either distinguish himself with a heroic deed or die in the mead-hall. Pleased, Wealhtheow takes her seat next to Hrothgar.

When night falls, the Danes leave the hall to Beowulf and his men. Beowulf lays aside his weapons and removes his armor, restating his intention to fight Grendel unarmed. He says that he considers himself to be as dangerous as Grendel. Beowulf lies down to wait, while his fearful men lie awake, doubting that any of them will live to see morning. In the dark night outside the hall, Grendel approaches stealthily, creeping toward the small band of Geats.

ANALYSIS

The two digressions in this section—Hrothgar's story of his former association with Beowulf's father and Beowulf's story of his swimming match against Breca—help to shed light on the main story by refining the reader's understanding of the Germanic heroic code of values. In Hrothgar's story of his previous association with Beowulf's father, we learn that there is a history of obligation between these two families. This anecdote explains the concept of the *wergild,* or "death-price," a set price that one pays, as Hrothgar did on Ecgtheow's behalf, to compensate the kin of anyone a warrior has killed. Paying the price of a man's life is the only way to keep the cycle of vengeance that characterizes a feud from continuing indefinitely. Such a payment replaces the volley of violent retaliation with an exchange of obligation. Thus Beowulf is at Heorot both to avenge the death of so many Danes at the hands of Grendel and also to discharge his father's debt to Hrothgar.

Interestingly, up until this point of the poem, Beowulf's decision to come to Hrothgar's aid has been described by the narrator as a heroic act of Beowulf's own deciding rather than an act of obligation or a payment of debt. When Beowulf explains his visit to the Danish coast guard, he again presents his journey as one made of his own free will. He doesn't respond directly to Hrothgar's story about Ecgtheow, perhaps wanting to bolster his claim that he has come seeking the monster of his own volition, not because he owes Hrothgar on behalf of his father. The second digression, Beowulf's account of his swimming match against his childhood companion Breca, comes when Unferth challenges Beowulf's heroic status. As there were no witnesses to Beowulf's exploits, his story cannot be corroborated. Beowulf can respond only with a series of elaborate boasts about his doings to preserve his honor. Throughout *Beowulf,* boasting is presented as a key component of one's reputation, a valid way to assert one's position in a hierarchy determined by deeds of valor. Beowulf's boasting, which especially pleases Wealhtheow, actually increases his honor and raises the level of expectations—for both those around him and the reader—as to how he will fare in the impending battle with Grendel.

But such boasting is a delicate social operation, and this scene helps to clarify the difference between proper and petulant boastfulness. Feeling upstaged by Beowulf, Unferth calls Beowulf's exploits foolhardy and accuses him of vanity. But it is Unferth himself who is guilty of vanity, since he is jealous of Beowulf. Etiquette dictates that it is inappropriate for Unferth to attempt to dishonor a guest; once he does, however, Beowulf's retaliation is appropriate and even necessary to maintain his reputation. Hrothgar's behavior, by contrast, is more dignified. He acknowledges that there is a certain "humiliation" in the fact that the Danes cannot solve their own problems, but he does not allow this disgrace to make him resentful of the superior warrior who has come to help (although one can argue that his assertion that Beowulf owes him on behalf of Ecgtheow helps him lessen his embarrassment at having to ask for help).

Reading closely, we find that the story that Beowulf tells is communalist in spite of its boastful tone. He depicts the culture of competition in which he and Breca were raised as fraternal and respectful, not vain and obsessive as Unferth would have it. Though he makes a sharp stab at Unferth when he points out his ineffectuality against Grendel, Beowulf ends his oration with a beautiful image of restored peace and happiness for his hosts, the Danes. Beowulf's correction thus not only better represents the true values of the society but also illustrates the proper way to tell a story. His story is more in keeping with the values of the code of honor than is Unferth's bitter speech.

LINES 710-1007

SUMMARY

Gleefully imagining the destruction that he will wreak, Grendel bursts into Heorot. He tears the door from its hinges with his bare hands and immediately devours a Geatish warrior while Beowulf carefully observes. When Grendel reaches out to snatch up Beowulf, he is stunned to find his arm gripped with greater strength than he knew possible. Terrified like a cornered animal, Grendel longs to run back to the safety of the swamplands. He tries to escape, but Beowulf wrestles him down. The combatants crash around the hall, rattling the walls and smashing the mead-benches. Grendel begins to shriek in pain and fear; the sound terrifies all who hear it. Beowulf's men heroically hack at the demon as Beowulf fights with him, but no weapon on earth is capable of harming Grendel. Beowulf summons even greater strength and rips Grendel's arm completely out of its socket. Fatally wounded, Grendel slinks back to his swampy home to die. Back in the mead-hall, Beowulf holds up his gory trophy in triumph. He proudly hangs the arm high on the wall of Heorot as proof of his victory.

The following morning, the Danish warriors are amazed at Beowulf's accomplishment. They race around on horseback in celebration, following the tracks of Grendel's retreat to the marshes. Beowulf's renown begins to spread rapidly. A Danish bard sings Beowulf's story to honor him and also recites the story of Sigemund, a great hero who slew a terrible dragon. The dragon was the guardian of a treasure hoard, which Sigemund won by slaying the dragon. The bard also sings of, and contrasts Beowulf with, Heremod, an evil Danish king who turned against his own people.

Hrothgar enters the mead-hall to see the trophy. He thanks God for finally granting him relief from Grendel. He then praises Beowulf, promises him lavish rewards, and says that he has adopted the warrior in his heart as a son. Beowulf receives Hrothgar's gratitude with modesty, expressing disappointment that he did not kill Grendel in the hall so that all could have seen the demon's corpse. The narrator mentions that the trophy arm, which seems to be made of "barbed steel," has disproved Unferth's claims of Beowulf's weakness. Order is restored in Heorot, and all the Danes begin to repair the great hall, which has been almost completely destroyed.

ANALYSIS

Beowulf is divided into three main parts, each of which centers on the hero's struggle against a particular monster—first Grendel, then Grendel's mother, then the dragon. In Beowulf's bloody battle against Grendel, the first part of the story reaches its climax. The poet chooses to relate much of this struggle from Grendel's perspective rather than from Beowulf's, emphasizing the fear and pain that Beowulf inflicts upon the demon. This narrative technique makes Beowulf seem even more godlike; he seems to be an unstoppable heroic force. Throughout the fight, Beowulf is treated as more than human. He shows himself stronger and more powerful than even the monstrous Grendel, and he seems completely invulnerable. It is never entirely clear what kind of being Grendel actually is—he is described as a demon, fiend, spirit, and stranger (in the Middle Ages, the word *monster* was used to describe birth defects; Grendel is later referred to as "an unnatural birth" [1353]). In any case, he seems to be a horrific beast, a large and distorted creature of vaguely human shape. His supernatural monstrousness makes Beowulf's conquest of him all the more impressive.

Many readers believe that each of the three monsters in the book has a symbolic or allegorical significance. The narrator seems to present Grendel as a representation of evil in the abstract. He can also, however, be interpreted as an evil force lurking within the Danish society itself. The theological implications of his descent from Cain support such an interpretation. The Old Testament relates how God punished Cain for his murder of his brother Abel by cursing him to wander. Grendel, too, is cursed and wanders, "haunting the marches, marauding round the heath / and the desolate fens" (103–104). The "marches" are the borders, and in Old English Grendel is called a "mearc-stapa," or border-stepper (103). The poet's culture finds the borders of society threatening, and Grendel is presented as an outsider who has penetrated the boundaries. Since Hrothgar, like Grendel, established himself by conquering his neighbors, some critics see the marauding Grendel as the embodiment of the society's own sin come back to haunt it. The nature of his abode—a swampy, dark, womblike landscape—supports this interpretation. He seems to be an incarnation of evil created by the human conscience. Furthermore, it is important to note that Grendel and Beowulf forego weapons to engage in ferocious hand-to-hand combat. This clash is not a mere battle in a culture dominated by warfare but rather a more personal, primal conflict between equal, opposite forces.

The *Beowulf* poet's description of the scop, or bard, who sings Beowulf's praises after the defeat of Grendel shows that he clearly values good workmanship, both in objects and in poetry. The narrator emphasizes the craftsmanship of the bard's "well-fashioned lines," just as he tends to dwell on the skill with which weapons and armor are forged. The bard's stories of Sigemund and Heremod reflect on the greatness of Beowulf by comparison and contrast, respectively. The Sigemund episode relates a familiar story from Norse mythology, which foreshadows Beowulf's fight with the dragon in the third part of the epic. The evil king Heremod, who fails to fulfill the responsibilities of a lord to his people, represents Beowulf's opposite. By comparing Beowulf to a king, the scop anticipates Beowulf's destiny for the throne in Geatland.

Heremod also serves as a foil for Hrothgar. Hrothgar's speech on the morning after the combat attributes Beowulf's victory to God without detracting from Beowulf's personal glory. He feels himself to be bound in a "new connection" with Beowulf by this great act of service. His appreciation and dedication to Beowulf are manifest in his promises that Beowulf will have the honors and rewards that are the appropriate recompenses for faithful service to a powerful lord. Unlike Heremod, Hrothgar represents the dutiful ruler in every way. Consequently, the Danes' loyalty to Hrothgar doesn't abate even when they are celebrating and revering Beowulf: "there was no laying of blame on their lord, / the noble Hrothgar; he was a good king" (861–862).

LINES 1008-1250

SUMMARY
Hrothgar hosts a great banquet in honor of Beowulf. He bestows upon him weapons, armor, treasure, and eight of his finest horses. He then presents Beowulf's men with rewards and compensates the Geats with gold for the Geatish warrior that Grendel killed.

After the gifts have been distributed, the king's scop comes forward to sing the saga of Finn, which begins with the Danes losing a bloody battle to Finn, the king of the Frisians, a neighbor tribe to the Danes. The Danish leader, Hnaef, is killed in the combat. Recognizing their defeat, the Danes strike a truce with the Frisians and agree to live with them separately but under common rule and equal treatment. Hildeburh, a Danish princess who is married to Finn, is doubly grieved by the outcome of the battle: she orders that the corpses of her brother, the Danish leader Hnaef, and her son, a Frisian warrior, be burned on the same bier. The Danes, homesick and bitter, pass a long winter with the Frisians. When spring comes, they rise against their enemies. Finn is then defeated and slain, and his widow, Hildeburh, is returned to Denmark.

When the scop finishes recounting the saga, Wealhtheow enters, wearing a gold crown, and praises her children, Hrethric and Hrothmund. She says that when Hrothgar dies, she is certain that the children will be treated well by their older cousin, Hrothulf, until they come of age. She expresses her hope that Beowulf too will act as a friend to them and offer them protection and guidance. She presents Beowulf with a torque (a collar or necklace) of gold and a suit of mail armor, asking again that he guide her sons and treat them kindly.

That night, the warriors sleep in Heorot, unaware that a new danger lurks in the darkness outside the hall.

ANALYSIS

The bard's tale of the conflict between the Danes and the Frisians— the Finnsburg episode, as this poem-within-a-poem is commonly called—contains some of the most beautiful and resonant language in *Beowulf,* utilizing many devices characteristic of Anglo-Saxon poetry. One such device is deliberate, emphatic understatement, as in the lines, "Hildeburh had little cause / to credit the Jutes" (1070–1071), where the point is that, in fact, she has enormous cause to discredit them. Also prominent is the use of *kennings*— compound words that evoke, poetically and often metaphorically, specific ideas, such as such as "ring-giver" (1101) for *king* (a king being one who rewards his warriors with rings) and "sea-lanes" (1156) for *ocean.*

The Finnsburg episode relates loosely to *Beowulf*'s central narrative. Although it isn't relevant to the main plot, it invokes the idea of vengeance as a component of honor. The story also highlights a tension in the heroic code by presenting the point of view of the Danish princess Hildeburh. Married to the Frisian king but herself a daughter of the Danes, Hildeburh experiences a divided loyalty. She has a son fighting on one side and a brother on the other. Like many other women in the Germanic warrior culture depicted in *Beowulf,* Hildeburh functions as a "peace-pledge between

nations"—an epithet that the poet later applies to Wealhtheow
(2017). Through marriage, Hildeburh helps to forge a connection
between tribes. Of course, the practice of using women as peace
tools is problematic for the men too. Here an uncle and a nephew
are on opposing sides, even though their Germanic culture prizes
a particularly strong bond between a man and his sister's son. In
the Finnsburg episode peace proves untenable. Hildeburh must be
taken back to Denmark—the ties between the two groups must be
severed—before the conflict can rest.

The story also gives the reader a sense of the Anglo-Saxon idea of
wyrd, or fate, in which individuals conceive of themselves as directed
by necessity and a heroic code that compels them to act in certain
fixed ways. The strong discussion of fate in this section is ominous,
and the reader quickly gets the sense that the Danes and Geats are
a little too exuberant in their rejoicing over the defeat of Grendel.
The narrator compounds this troubling feeling by informing us that
a reversal of fortune is coming: "how could they know fate, / the
grim shape of things to come" (1233–1234). *Beowulf*'s plot often
anticipates itself in this manner. It may even seem to us as though the
narrator is giving away the plot and destroying the suspense. For the
Beowulf poet, however, the pull of fate is so strong that an event that
is *fated* to happen in the future already has a strong presence. Fate
walks among these characters whether they know it or not.

The narrator's tendency to project forward to future events manifests itself as well in his hints that Hrothulf, Hrothgar's nephew,
will usurp the throne from Hrothgar's sons. Wealhtheow's statement that she is certain of Hrothulf's goodness creates a moment
of dramatic irony, as the poet is well aware that Hrothulf has evil
in mind. The treachery related in the Finnsburg episode casts a
similarly ominous pall over Wealhtheow's speech and suggests that
treachery will mark the future just as it has the past. Such continuity is symbolized in the golden torque that Wealhtheow presents to
Beowulf. The poet's glance forward to Hygelac's death while wearing the torque (which Beowulf will have given him) reinforces how
symbols link the past, present, and future in this culture.

LINES 1251–1491

SUMMARY

*Wise sir, do not grieve. It is always better
to avenge dear ones than to indulge in mourning.*

(See QUOTATIONS, *p. 52*)

As the warriors sleep in the mead-hall, Grendel's mother, a horrible monster in her own right, descends on Heorot in a frenzy of grief and rage, seeking vengeance for her son's death. When she falls upon and seizes a sleeping man, the noise wakes the others. The warriors seize their swords and rush toward her. The monster panics and flees, still carrying her victim, Hrothgar's trusted adviser, Aeschere, in her grasp. Beowulf, having been given other sleeping quarters, is away from Heorot when Grendel's mother makes her raid. By the time he arrives at the hall, she is gone. The warriors discover that she has stolen Grendel's arm as well.

Devastated with grief over the loss of his friend and counselor, Hrothgar summons Beowulf and explains what has occurred. He entreats Beowulf to seek out and kill Grendel's mother, describing the horrible, swampy wood where she keeps her lair. The place has a magical quality. The water burns and the bottom of the mere, or lake, has never been reached. Even the animals seem to be afraid of the water there.

Hrothgar tells Beowulf that he must depend on him a second time to rid Heorot of a demon. He says that he will give him chests of gold if he rises to the challenge. Beowulf agrees to the fight, reassuring Hrothgar that Grendel's mother won't get away. The warriors mount up and ride into the fens, following the tracks of their enemy. When they reach a cliff's edge, they discover Aeschere's head lying on the ground. The scene below is horrifying: in the murky water, serpents and sea-dragons writhe and roil. Beowulf slays one beast with an arrow.

Beowulf, "indifferent to death," prepares himself for combat by donning his armor and girding himself with weapons (1442). Unferth loans him the great and seasoned sword Hrunting, which has never failed in any battle. Beowulf speaks, asking Hrothgar to take care of the Geats and return his property to Hygelac if he, Beowulf, should be killed. He also bequeaths his own sword to Unferth.

[His helmet] was of beaten gold,
princely headgear hooped and hasped
by a weapon-smith who had worked wonders.

(See QUOTATIONS, *p. 53)*

ANALYSIS

The intensity of the epic increases in these lines, as its second part begins with the arrival of Grendel's mother at the hall. The idea of the blood feud, which has been brought up earlier in the scop's stories and in Hrothgar's memory of the Wulfings' grudge against Ecgtheow, now enters the main plot. Just as Grendel's slaughter of Hrothgar's men requires avenging, so does Beowulf's slaying of Grendel. As Beowulf tells Hrothgar, in a speech with central importance to his conception of the heroic code of honor, "It is always better / to avenge dear ones than to indulge in mourning / . . . / When a warrior is gone, [glory] will be his best and only bulwark" (1384–1389). In this speech, Beowulf explicitly characterizes revenge as a means to fame and glory, which make reputations immortal. As this speech demonstrates, an awareness of death pervades *Beowulf*. That some aspect or memory of a person remains is therefore of great importance to the warriors. The world of the poem is harsh, dangerous, and unforgiving, and innumerable threats—foreign enemies, monsters, and natural perils—loom over every life.

One of the most interesting aspects of Grendel's mother's adherence to the same vengeance-demanding code as the warriors is that she is depicted as not wholly alien. Her behavior is not only comprehensible but also justified. In other ways, however, Grendel and his mother are indeed portrayed as creatures from another world. One aspect of their difference from the humans portrayed in the poem is that Grendel's strong parent figure is his *mother* rather than his father—his family structure that is out of keeping with the vigorously patriarchal society of the Danes and the Geats. As Hrothgar explains it, "They are fatherless creatures, / and their whole ancestry is hidden" (1355–1356). The idea of a hidden ancestry is obviously suspect and sinister in this society that places such a high priority—a sacredness, even—on publicizing and committing to memory one's lineage.

Grendel's relation to Cain has been mentioned at several points in the story and is revisited here. Having Cain for an ancestor is obviously a liability from the perspective of a culture obsessed with family loyalty. Grendel's lineage is therefore in many ways an unnatural one, demonic and accursed, since Cain brought murder, specifically murder of kin, into the world. As discussed earlier, it is possible to interpret Grendel and his mother, considering the unnaturalness of their existence, as the manifestation of some sort of psychological tension about the conquering and killing that dominate the Danish and the Geatish societies. Certainly, the humans' feud with the monsters seems to stand outside the normal culture of warfare and seems to carry a suggestion of moral and spiritual importance.

The question of Grendel's lineage is one of many examples of the *Beowulf* poet's struggle to resolve the tension between his own Christian worldview and the obviously pagan origins of his narrative. The narrative's origins lie in a pagan past, but by the time the poem was written down (sometime around 700 A.D.), almost all of the Anglo-Saxons had been converted to Christianity. The Scandinavian settings and characters thus would have been distant ancestral memories for the inhabitants of England, as the migrations from Scandinavia and Germany had taken place centuries earlier. Throughout the epic, the poet makes references to this point and tries to reconcile the behavior of his characters with a Christian system of belief that often seems alien to the action of the poem. Early on, for example, he condemns the Danes' journeys to pagan shrines, where they make offerings, hoping to rid themselves of Grendel. Additionally, Beowulf's heroic exploits are constantly framed in terms of God's role in them, as though Beowulf owes all of his abilities to providence—an idea that hardly seems compatible with the earthly boasting and reputation-building with which he occupies himself throughout the poem. The conflict between the Anglo-Saxon idea of fate (*wyrd*) and the Christian God was probably a widespread moral tension in the poet's time, and it animates *Beowulf* from beginning to end.

Lines 1492–1924

Summary

> *Choose, dear Beowulf, the better part,*
> *eternal rewards. Do not give way to pride.*
> (See QUOTATIONS, p. 54)

Beowulf swims downward for the better part of a day before he sees the bottom. As he nears the murky lake floor, Grendel's mother senses his approach. She lunges at him and clutches him in his grip, but his armor, as predicted, prevents her from crushing him. She drags Beowulf to her court, while a mass of sea-monsters claws and bites at him. Beowulf wields Hrunting, the sword lent to him by Unferth, and lashes at Grendel's mother's head, but even the celebrated blade of Hrunting is unable to pierce the monster's skin. Beowulf tries to fight the sea-witch using only his bare hands, but she matches him blow for blow. At last, he notices a sword hanging on the wall, an enormous weapon forged for giants. Beowulf seizes the huge sword and swings it in a powerful arc. The blade slices cleanly through the Grendel's mother's neck, and she falls dead to the floor, gushing with blood. The hero is exultant. A light appears, and Beowulf looks around, his sword held high in readiness. He spies Grendel's corpse lying in a corner. Furious at the sight of the fiend, he decapitates Grendel as a final repayment for all of the lives that Grendel took.

On land, the Danes lose hope when they see blood well up from the depths. Sure that their champion is lost, they return to Heorot in sorrow. Only the small band of Geats, Beowulf's kinsmen, waits on.

Back in the monster's court, the blade of the giant's sword begins to melt, burned by Grendel's fiery blood. Beowulf seizes its hilt, which remains solid and, grasping Grendel's head in his other hand, swims for the surface. He finds that the waters he passes through are no longer infested now that the demon has been destroyed. When he breaks the surface, the Geats are overjoyed as they advance to meet him and unfasten his armor.

The group returns to Heorot in triumph. Four men impale the heavy head of Grendel on a spear and lug it between them. When they arrive at the hall, the Danes gawk at the head in horror and amazement. Beowulf presents the head and the sword hilt to Hrothgar, assuring him of his future security. Hrothgar praises Beowulf's goodness, evenness, and loyalty, contrasts him with the evil King Heremod, and predicts a great future for him. He delivers a long speech about how to be a good and wise ruler by choosing eternal rather than earthly rewards. Hrothgar then promises to shower Beowulf with treasure the following morning.

Another banquet ensues, with great feasting and revelry. Afterward, Beowulf retires to get some much-needed rest. In the morning, he has Hrunting returned to Unferth and tells Hrothgar that he and his men long to return home to Geatland. Hrothgar praises Beowulf again, saying that he has united the Geats and the Danes in ties of friendship and loyalty. He presents Beowulf with twelve treasures. Despite his urgings that Beowulf return to Denmark soon, Hrothgar knows that he will never see Beowulf again. The Geats return to the coast, where they grant a reward to the watchman who has guarded their ship. They then sail back to Geatland and return to the hall of Hygelac.

ANALYSIS

Many readers have pondered the significance of Grendel and his mother—whether they are part of the same evil force or represent two separate ideas. Earlier, after Grendel's defeat, there are frequent suggestions, even amid the celebration, that the evil that Grendel represents has not been stamped out. These hints may lead the reader to suspect that Grendel himself is still alive—though Beowulf rips his arm off, we never actually see Grendel die, and Beowulf regrets letting him get away. That the remaining threat proves instead to be the monster's mother suggests, perhaps, that although an instance of evil has been eliminated with Grendel, the evil must still be eradicated at its source—Grendel's mother might be thought of as representing a more foundational or primordial evil than Grendel himself. On the other hand, there is less theological language attached to her malice than to Grendel's. She seems to be more unambiguously animalistic and less a symbol of pure evil than he is. For example, her attack on Heorot is even appropriate and honorable by the standards of the warrior culture, as it marks an attempt to avenge her son's death.

This second encounter prompts a change of scene in the poem, drawing the hero out of the safety of the mead-hall and into the dark, alien, suggestive world of his adversaries. The advantage of fighting on familiar terrain within the boundaries of human society—an advantage that Beowulf enjoys in his encounter against Grendel—is now lost. This time, Beowulf must struggle against a resistant natural environment in addition to a ferocious monster. The reader already has been prepared for Beowulf's superhuman swimming abilities by the earlier story of the contest with Breca. However, the mere, or lake, in which Grendel's mother lives is no ordinary body of water. It teems with blood and gore, as well as with unsavory creatures of all descriptions. It is an elemental world of water, fire, and blood, and one with an extremely unholy feel to it.

Imagery of darkness and light is important in this underwater world. The darkness of the lair symbolizes evil, and it leads to Beowulf's general disorientation in this unfamiliar environment.

The first glimmer of light that he sees signifies his arrival at the very heart and hearth of this den of terror. Once he defeats Grendel's mother, her lair is illuminated more thoroughly: "A light appeared and the place brightened / the way the sky does when heaven's candle / is shining clearly" (1570–1572). Because light bears the implication of Christian holiness and salvation, with these words, the poet suggests that hell has been purged of its evil and sanctity restored. Additionally, it seems clear that by the time Beowulf gets back onto land, he has undergone a sort of rebirth, a transition from a brave but somewhat reckless warrior into a wise and steadfast leader. Indeed, the remainder of this section is dominated by elaborate formal oratory detailing the characteristics of successful participation in society. In particular, Beowulf receives earnest advice from Hrothgar, by now a father-figure, about how to comport himself both as a man and as a ruler.

LINES 1925–2210

SUMMARY

Beowulf and his men return to the magnificent hall of King Hygelac and to Queen Hygd, who is beautiful and wise, though very young. The narrator tells the story of the legendary Queen Modthryth, who "perpetrated terrible wrongs" against her subjects, torturing and even killing many innocent people who she imagined were offending her. Modthryth's behavior improved, we are told, once she was married to the great king of the Angles, Offa.

Beowulf and his men approach the hall, where the Geats, who have heard that their hero has returned, are preparing for his arrival. Hygelac extends a formal greeting while Hygd pours mead for the warriors. Hygelac asks Beowulf how he fared in the land of Hrothgar, recalling that he had known that Beowulf's task would be a fearsome one and that he had advised Beowulf not to face such a dangerous foe.

Beowulf begins his tale by describing the courteous treatment that he received from Hrothgar and Wealhtheow. He then prophesies an unhappy outcome to the peace-weaving engagement of Freawaru, Hrothgar's daughter, to Ingeld the Heathobard. He predicts that the sight of the ancestral possessions of each worn by the kin of the other (the result of many years of warring and plundering) will cause memories of the deep and lengthy feud between the Danes and the Heathobards to surface, so that they will not be able to keep themselves from continuing to fight.

Beowulf then tells the story of his encounter with Grendel. He particularly emphasizes the monster's ferocity and the rewards that he received from Hrothgar. He relates the battle with Grendel's mother as well. He then presents his king with a large part of the treasure given to him by Hrothgar, including suits of armor and four of the great horses. He gives Hygd a priceless necklace—the torque given him by Wealhtheow—and three horses. Beowulf is praised throughout Geatland for his valorous deeds and courteousness. Hygelac gives him a great deal of treasure and land of his own to rule.

In time, Hygelac is killed in battle with the Shylfings, and the kingdom falls to Beowulf. For fifty years he rules the Geats, becoming a great and wise king.

ANALYSIS

This transitional section returns Beowulf to his homeland and introduces us briefly to his king and queen, Hygelac and Hygd. Like Wealhtheow in Denmark, Hygd is presented as a positive example of proper behavior in women—she is gracious in bearing and manner, attentive to the men around her, and loyal to her husband and lord. In order to highlight these positive qualities, the poet positions the legendarily wicked Queen Modthryth as Hygd's foil (a character whose traits contrast with and thereby accentuate those of another character). *Beowulf* is set in a highly male-dominated world—perhaps one even more male-dominated than that of Homer's *Iliad*—governed by violence, honor, and doom. In this culture, women are seen as marriageable objects, links between warring tribes to achieve peace (Wealhtheow is referred to as "peace-pledge between nations" [2017]).

Beowulf is clearly skeptical about the power of marriage to heal the anger and hatred generated between blood enemies. His dire predictions about the marriage of Hrothgar's daughter, Freawaru, to an enemy clansman, Heathobard, reveal his belief that the desire for vengeance will always overcome the peace that intermarriage attempts to establish. The events of the Finnsburg episode, in which the marriage-tie was quickly violated and the bride returned to her kinsmen, seem to validate this sentiment. In any case, this detail about the engagement of Hrothgar's daughter and its political context is one of several new elements that Beowulf's retelling introduces, keeping the story from becoming too repetitive.

Beowulf's pessimistic speculations about this union add to the discourse on treasure that has been running throughout the poem. His argument that some ancestral item will catch a family member's eye and renew the feud seems valid—we have seen that many items of treasure, such as the various swords and the necklace that Wealhtheow gives Beowulf, are in fact heirlooms, loaded with symbolic and memorial significance. Thus, Freawaru, as a peace-pledge, is pitted against treasure, which has the potential to rekindle bad memories and feuds.

In his retelling of his experiences in Denmark, Beowulf emphasizes the treasure that he has won as much as the poet does in his narration of the events. Throughout *Beowulf*, a tension manifests itself between the pagan regard for treasure as a symbol of personal valor and the Christian conception of treasure as a symbol of sinful greed. As we have seen, treasure is directly related to success in war and an accumulation of treasure signifies an accumulation of honor. Most important, the treasure must continue to be redistributed. In this sense, Hrothgar is a good king because he is such a generous "ring-giver" and Beowulf a good retainer because he gives Hygelac and Hygd more than half of his rewards. The poem's Christian undertones, however, focus on earthly possessions as unimportant. For example, after Beowulf slays Grendel's mother, Hrothgar advises Beowulf to "[c]hoose . . . the better part, / eternal rewards," warning him, essentially, not to rest on the laurels of his conquests (1759–1760).

This section also further develops the image of the mead-hall as an important element in Anglo-Saxon warrior culture. Hygelac's hall in Geatland proves just as magnificent and just as important a place of sanctuary and reward in a world where danger lurks on every horizon as Heorot, the great hall of the Danes. In the mead-hall, boasts can be made, jokes can be exchanged, and the idea of doom can be postponed. It is in the mead-hall that warriors can revel in the glory and the reputations that they risk such peril to win.

The ceremonies in Hygelac's hall seem to reflect a growing intimacy between Beowulf and the king, his uncle, as well as a growing respect for a warrior who had previously been undervalued, as we now learn for the first time: "[Beowulf] had been poorly regarded / for a long time" (2183–2184). Thus, the retelling in the mead-hall of Beowulf's heroic deeds—a retelling that may seem anticlimactic to many readers—is an important political moment for Beowulf and an important step in his advancement from warrior to ruler.

LINES 2211–2515

SUMMARY

Soon it is Geatland's turn to face terror. A great dragon lurks beneath the earth, jealously guarding its treasure, until one day a thief manages to infiltrate the barrow, or mound, where the treasure lies. The thief steals a gem-covered goblet, arousing the wrath of the dragon. The intruder, a slave on the run from a hard-handed master, intends no harm by his theft and flees in a panic with the goblet.

The poet relates that many centuries earlier, the last survivor of an ancient race buried the treasure in the barrow when he realized that the treasure would be of no use to him because he, like his ancestors, was destined to die. He carefully buried the precious objects, lamenting all the while his lonely state. The defeat of his people had left the treasures to deteriorate. The dragon chanced upon the hoard and has been guarding it for the past three hundred years.

Waking up to find the goblet stolen, the dragon bursts forth from the barrow to hunt the thief, scorching the earth as it travels. Not finding the offender, the dragon goes on a rampage, breathing fire and incinerating homes and villages. It begins to emerge nightly from its barrow to torment the countryside, still seething with rage at the theft.

Soon, Beowulf's own throne-hall becomes the target of the dragon's fiery breath, and it is burned to the ground. Now an old king, Beowulf grieves and wonders what he might have done to deserve such punishment from God. He begins to plot his revenge. He commissions a mighty shield from the iron-smith, one that he hopes will stand up against the breath of flame. He is too proud to assemble a huge army for the fight, and, remembering how he defeated Grendel single-handedly in his youth, feels no fear of the dragon.

The poet recounts the death of King Hygelac in combat in Friesland. Hygelac fell while Beowulf survived thanks to his great strength and swimming ability. Upon returning home, Beowulf was offered the throne by the widowed Hygd, who knew that her own son was too young and inexperienced to be an effective ruler. Beowulf declined, however, not wanting to disturb the order of succession. Instead, he acted as protector and guardian to the prince and supported his rule. Only when Hygelac's son met his end in a skirmish against the Swedes did Beowulf ascend the throne. Under Beowulf's reign, the feuding with Sweden eventually ceased when Beowulf avenged Hygelac's death.

Now, ready to face one last adversary, Beowulf gathers eleven men to investigate the area. They discover the thief who stole the dragon's goblet and press him to take them to the barrow. They wish each other luck in the fight that will follow, and Beowulf has a premonition of his own death. On the cliff outside the barrow, Beowulf speaks to his men, recounting his youth as a ward in King Hrethel's court. He tells of the accidental killing of one of Hrethel's sons by another and attempts to characterize the king's great grief. He describes the wars between the Geats and the Swedes after Hrethel's death, recalling his proud days as a warrior in the service of Hygelac. He then makes his final boast: he vows to fight the dragon, if only it will abandon its barrow and face him on open ground.

ANALYSIS

This section moves us into the third part of the poem, which centers around the aged Beowulf's fight with the dragon. From beginning to end, the tone of this section is one of death and doom. The unknown ancestor who buries the treasure, for example, behaves as mournfully as if he were actually burying his deceased kinsmen—or, indeed, himself. Also, there are repeated hints that Beowulf will not survive this encounter. Much of this section is retrospective and nostalgic, as Beowulf, sensing that his end is near, feels compelled to rehearse the story of his distinguished life.

The emphasis on the treasure itself in this section rehashes the moral ambiguity of materialism caused by the overlaying of a Christian value system on a pagan story. As translator Seamus Heaney points out in his introduction, the idea of gold in the Sigemund episode is associated almost entirely with goodness and honor, while here it is also associated with greed, theft, evil, and death. But the anecdote of the Last Survivor, which tells how the gold came to be buried in the barrow, demonstrates a different ethos. The survivor seems to realize that the treasure is meaningless without a community in which to circulate. This realization isn't exactly a Christian lesson in the transience of earthly things, since no alternative spiritual world is proposed; neither, however, does it reflect a greedy, purely materialistic lust for gold. In this anecdote, the *Beowulf* poet seems to have given the pagan ethos a fairly sympathetic and even-handed treatment.

The lengthy passages of recapitulation and reminiscence fill in the details of Beowulf's political biography. In the previous section, the reader learns only that Beowulf came to the throne after Hygelac's death and ruled for fifty years. Now, however, we find out about a significant gesture of generosity on Beowulf's part toward Hygelac's son. By declining the throne and taking on the guardianship of the young heir until the heir comes of age, Beowulf shows that his attitude toward power is neither ambitious nor mercenary. He thus stands in contrast to the power-hungry usurper Hrothulf. In proclaiming of Beowulf that "He was a good king," the poet echoes his praise of the venerable Shield Sheafson and of Hrothgar (2390).

The tragic story of the death of Hrethel's son at the hands of his own brother offers an echo of the earlier case of divided loyalty in the Finnsburg episode. There, the Danish princess Hildeburh was distressed by the fact that her son and her brother were at war, fighting on opposite sides, and that ultimately both were killed. Here, the tension is similar but even more frustrating. Hrethel's grief at the accident is great, but because of the peculiar circumstances surrounding his son's death, Hrethel is locked in inaction. Under the heroic code, grief is something to be purged through vengeance, but vengeance here would mean the death of another son—an excruciating and unsatisfying prospect.

The circumstances surrounding and leading up to Beowulf's confrontation with the dragon prepare us for a climactic spectacle. The poet has aligned Beowulf with the force of good throughout the story, and the dragon's direct attack on Beowulf's hall renders this imminent encounter an inevitable clash between good and evil. The contrast drawn between Hrothgar, who earlier calls on the young Beowulf to eradicate Grendel, and the now old Beowulf, who enlists no such help against the dragon, accentuates Beowulf's valor and instills in us a confidence that Beowulf is still mighty enough to eradicate a menacing foe. The poet's explicit comparison between Hygelac, who died, and Beowulf, who lived, in the combat in Friesland similarly builds our expectations that Beowulf will succeed in his quest.

Yet Beowulf's premonition of his own death attests to his strong sense of fate, an important component of these characters' self-conceptions. Beowulf's reminiscences about his glory days and the narrator's mention of Beowulf's old age reinforce the reality that every life—even that of a legendary warrior—must come to an end. Thus, the poem gives us the feeling that this clash can end only in total destruction. Beowulf's call for the dragon to face him on open ground has the same primal feel to it as his youthful decision to fight Grendel unarmed. Whereas the earlier clash establishes Beowulf's reputation as a hero, we know this last clash must seal Beowulf's heroic reputation forever.

LINES 2516–2820

SUMMARY

Beowulf bids farewell to his men and sets off wearing a mail-shirt and a helmet to fight the dragon. He shouts a challenge to his opponent, who emerges from the earth. Man and dragon grapple and wrestle amid sheets of fire. Beowulf hacks with his sword against the dragon's thick scales, but his strength is clearly not what it once was. As the flames billow, Beowulf's companions run in terror. Only one, Wiglaf, feels enough loyalty to come to the aid of his king. Wiglaf chides the other warriors, reminding them of their oaths of loyal service to Beowulf. Now the time has come when their loyalty will be tested, Wiglaf declares, and he goes by himself to assist his lord.

Beowulf strikes the dragon in the head with his great sword Naegling, but the sword snaps and breaks. The dragon lands a bite on Beowulf's neck, and blood begins to flow. Wiglaf rushes to Beowulf's aid, stabbing the dragon in the belly, and the dragon scorches Wiglaf's hand. In desperation Beowulf pulls a knife from his belt and stabs it deep into the dragon's flank. The blow is fatal, and the writhing serpent withers. But no sooner has Beowulf triumphed than the wound on his neck begins to burn and swell. He realizes that the dragon bite is venomous and that he is dying. He sends Wiglaf to inspect the dragon's treasure and bring him a portion of it, saying that death will be easier if he sees the hoard that he has liberated. Wiglaf descends into the barrow and quickly returns to Beowulf with an armload of treasure. The old king, dying, thanks God for the treasure that he has won for his people. He tells Wiglaf that he must now look after the Geats and order his troop to build him a barrow that people will call "Beowulf's Barrow." After giving Wiglaf the collar from his own neck, Beowulf dies.

ANALYSIS

The dragon is the poem's most potent symbol, embodying the idea of *wyrd*, or fate, that imbues the story with an atmosphere of doom and death. Whereas Beowulf is essentially invulnerable to Grendel and his mother, he is in danger from the beginning against the dragon. As Beowulf feels his own death approaching, the dragon emerges from the earth, creating the feeling that the inevitable clash will result in Beowulf's death. The poet emphasizes Beowulf's reluctance to meet death, to "give ground like that and go / unwillingly to inhabit another home / in a place beyond" (2588–2590). This poetic evocation of death as constituting movement from one realm to another—from the earthly realm to the spiritual one—reveals the influence of Christian ideology on the generally pagan *Beowulf*. It is also poignant from the perspective of the warrior ethos, in which leaving one's homeland, the anchor of one's entire identity, is a very serious and significant undertaking.

That Beowulf should be so adamant in his desire to see the treasure before he dies has puzzled many readers. It is important to remember that treasure objects often function as symbols of the transmission of values through generations or of bonds of kinship and loyalty. Beowulf recognizes this symbolic function when he reflects that he would pass on his armor to his own son if he had one. His relief upon seeing the treasure demonstrates his desire to leave something to his people—a sort of surrogate offspring—when he dies. He knows that, even though he has slain the dragon, his victory will feel hollow if there is no subsequent enactment of the ritual of reward and gift-giving. Looking upon the treasure—ensuring himself of its physical reality—eases Beowulf's mind before death.

That the treasure that Wiglaf finds is rusty and corroded, however, adds a pathetic, ironic quality to the scene. Whereas Beowulf's first two encounters with monsters end with him being granted treasures whose splendor represents his valor, the final encounter ends with Beowulf clutching objects whose decaying state epitomizes his own proximity to death. Furthermore, these riches will be entombed with Beowulf, so that the treasure will be hoarded, in effect, rather than redistributed, as the heroic code normally demands. In a way, Beowulf is like the original burier of the treasure, who realized that he was the last of his line—he knows that his lineage will not continue. Because the nature of Beowulf's fight with the dragon is so different from that of his fights with Grendel and his mother, some critics choose to see the poem as having a dipartite, or two-part, structure rather than a tri-partite one. In the first two fights, we see a warrior confident in his indestructibility; in the last fight, on the other hand, we see a warrior aware of his mortality.

The treasure also stands for the growing bond between Beowulf and Wiglaf, the old hero and the new. Of Beowulf's men, Wiglaf is the only one who conforms to the heroic standards of loyalty and valor. Wiglaf, in this section, establishes himself as the legitimate successor to Beowulf, who has no natural heir. In this way, he is similar to the young Beowulf, who becomes Hrothgar's adoptive son. Wiglaf fiercely swears that he would rather die than return home without having protected his leader. This vow, too, reminds us of the young Beowulf, who is so eloquent in enunciating the code of honor and so perfectly epitomizes its values. The continuity of honor from one generation to the next is ratified when Beowulf takes the collar of gold from his own neck and, as his final act, gives it to his young friend. In Old English, a *laf* is an heirloom or remnant, and Wiglaf means "war survivor." The poet equates Wiglaf with the treasure (and, of course, the poem)—he will survive Beowulf's lifetime and carry on the great hero's legacy.

LINES 2821–3182

SUMMARY

Beowulf lies dead, and Wiglaf is bowed down with grief at the loss of his lord. The dragon, too, lies slain on the ground. The poet briefly commemorates the beast's end. Slowly, the Geatish warriors who had fled from the battle straggle back to the barrow to find Wiglaf still vainly trying to revive their fallen leader. The men are ashamed, and Wiglaf rebukes them bitterly, declaring that all of Beowulf's generosity has been wasted on them. The cost of their cowardice, he predicts, will be greater than just the life of a great ruler. He suggests that foreign warlords will be sure to attack the Geats now that Beowulf can no longer protect them.

Wiglaf sends a messenger with tidings to the Geats, who wait nervously for news of the outcome of the battle. The messenger tells them of Beowulf's death and warns them that the hostile Franks and the Frisians will most certainly attack them. He expresses concern about the Swedes as well, who have a long-held grudge against the Geats; he relates the history of their feud and tells how the Geats secured the last victory. Without Beowulf to protect them, the messenger predicts, the Geats risk invasion by Swedes. The poet confirms that many of the messenger's predictions will prove true.

The Geats then rise and go to Beowulf's body. They discover also the fearsome, fifty-foot-long corpse of the dragon. It is revealed that the hoard had been under a spell, so that no person could open it except by the will of God. Wiglaf recounts Beowulf's last requests and readies the people to build his funeral pyre. With seven of the greatest Geatish thanes, Wiglaf returns to the dragon's bier to collect the treasure that Beowulf bought with his life. They hurl the dragon's body into the water.

The pyre is built high and decked with armor, according to Beowulf's wishes. The body is laid in and the fire is lit—its roar competes with the sound of weeping. A Geatish woman laments Beowulf's death and grieves about the war-torn future that she foresees for her people. The Geats place Beowulf's remains on a cliff high above the sea in a barrow that will be visible to all passing ships. Sorrowfully, they recount that their king was kind and generous to his people, fair-minded, and eager to earn praise.

ANALYSIS
The conclusion of the epic begins with a brief but lovely elegiac passage in honor of the dragon, consigning it, along with Beowulf, to the company of those who can no longer exercise their greatness. The poet emphasizes the dragon's beauty and grace of movement ("Never again would he glitter and glide" [2832]), illustrating that the beast was magnificent in its own right and a worthy match for the great hero. The poet's admiring words about the dragon glorify Beowulf's feat in slaying such a creature and demonstrate a respect for the slain enemy that Grendel and his mother never enjoyed. The poet here demonstrates his sensitivity to balance—what the translator calls "four-squareness"—as he dwells on the two bodies lying side by side, two remarkable lives come to a close. The symmetry and pacing in this nostalgic moment help to prepare us for the elaborate ceremony of the funeral with which the poem concludes. Of course, the first foreshadowing of Beowulf's funeral comes much earlier, with the recounting of the death of Shield Sheafson at the beginning of the poem. The story has now come full circle.

Wiglaf's rebuke of his fellow warriors, along with the messenger's prophecy about Geatland's imminent troubles, offers a great deal of insight into the importance of the warrior-king figure in early feudal societies. In a world where small societies are constantly at war over land, wealth, resources, and honor, the presence of a powerful king is essential to the safety and well-being of a people. When a king dies, his people become vulnerable to the marauding forces beyond their borders. The doom that hangs over the entire narration of Beowulf's story seems to descend swiftly upon his people the moment that he dies, and the wailing Geats are well aware of what the lack of Beowulf's protection means for them. Wiglaf suggests as well that the weakness and deficiency of his fellow warriors will encourage invaders. The Geats have sacrificed their reputation as valiant warriors by refusing to come to the aid of their king, and reputation is itself an important layer of defense. Once word of their cowardice gets out, they will surely become targets of attack.

By the time of the funeral, Wiglaf's initial rage against his compatriots has cooled somewhat, and he speaks once more for the community. As extensively as it honors Beowulf's greatness, the final scene of the poem comes closer than any other to criticizing his behavior. Wiglaf reflects that there may have been an element of irresponsibility in Beowulf's single-mindedness and daring when he proclaims, "Often when one man follows his own will / many are hurt. This happened to us" (3077–3078). This declaration, in conjunction with the earlier statement that Beowulf was too proud to field a large army against the dragon, suggests that his actions were not wholly courageous but also, to a degree, foolhardy and headstrong. Like Wiglaf, we are left to ponder how courage can balance with judgment to yield true heroism.

The issue of the cursed treasure compounds the ambiguity surrounding the meaning of Beowulf's death. The poet's assertion that the ancient warrior acted wrongly in burying the gold underground suggests that Beowulf is the God-chosen liberator of the imprisoned wealth. Though Beowulf approaches the matter of the treasure unselfishly, wishing to free his people from the menace of the dragon, his death nevertheless seems something of a punishment. Ultimately, however, in a culture of heroism—in which so much emphasis is placed on virtue, in which warriors would rather die than live in shame—the noble funeral that Beowulf receives validates his choices in life. The poem *Beowulf* exemplifies this culture's emphasis on memorializing departed heroes; indeed, the mere existence of the poem itself is a testament to Beowulf's virtue and the esteem his people placed upon him.

IMPORTANT QUOTATIONS
EXPLAINED

1. So. The Spear-Danes in days gone by
   and the kings who ruled them had courage and greatness.
   . . .
   There was Shield Sheafson, scourge of many tribes,
   a wrecker of mead-benches, rampaging among foes.
   . . .
   A foundling to start with, he would flourish later on
   . . .
   In the end each clan on the outlying coasts
   beyond the whale-road had to yield to him
   and begin to pay tribute. That was one good king.

   (1–11)

These lines, which open the poem, establish the highly stylized nature of Seamus Heaney's translation and set forth some of the poem's central ideas. Heaney's choice to translate the first word of the poem as "So" has been much remarked upon. It had previously been translated into such poetic-sounding invocations as "Hark" and "Lo" or, more casually, "Listen." In his introduction, Heaney explains his choice by pointing out that "so," in the speech of his Ulster relatives, "operates as an expression which obliterates all previous discourse and narrative, and at the same time functions as an exclamation calling for immediate attention." From the outset, then, the poem whips us into its world while maintaining an inviting, conversational tone.

Heaney's translation re-creates many of the conventions of Anglo-Saxon poetry. He breaks his lines into two halves with a strong caesura, or pause, wherever possible (lines 4, 5, and 11, for example). Second, he uses alliteration, or repetition of consonant sounds, across the caesura to bind the two half-lines together through sound ("foundling . . . flourish"). He also replicates the *Beowulf* poet's extensive use of multiple names or phrases for a single person, group, or idea; thus Shield Sheafson, in the space of two lines, is referred to as "scourge of many tribes" and "wrecker of mead-benches." Finally, the compound word "whale-road," used here to refer to the sea, is one of the most famous examples of the Anglo-Saxon rhetorical figure called the *kenning*, which replaces a noun with a metaphorical description of the noun.

In addition to these stylistic features, the opening lines also introduce a number of thematic ideas that prove important throughout the poem. The poet's presentation of the ancestor Shield Sheafson as the model of heroism is representative of the poem's obsession with patriarchal history. Characters are constantly defined in terms of their fathers and ancestors. This passage also emphasizes heroic action itself as a cultural value—even a fatherless individual can make a name for himself if he behaves like a hero. Thus, the orphan Shield Sheafson earned an immutable reputation as "one good king" by the end of his life. The great force of reputation will also continue to be an important theme. By establishing fame in his lifetime, an individual can hope to be remembered by subsequent generations—the only consolation that death affords.

QUOTATIONS

2.   And a young prince must be prudent like that,
giving freely while his father lives
so that afterwards in age when fighting starts
steadfast companions will stand by him
and hold the line. Behaviour that's admired
is the path to power among people everywhere.

(20–25)

This excerpt, which expounds the virtues of the early Danish king Beow, illustrates the kind of political prudence that characterizes Hrothgar, who is a descendant of Beow. The heroic code's system of loyalties entails a very specific political and diplomatic structure. Generosity is valued greatly in a king, but there is no attempt to disguise the fact that it is motivated by the need to maintain the support of a band of retainers. The warrior culture accepts and embraces this give-and take relationship between ruler and ruled as necessary for society to function effectively. The emphasis on the loyalty of the warriors ("when fighting starts / steadfast companions will stand by him") has a special resonance for Beowulf, given the disloyalty of his men in his encounter with the dragon.

This passage also emphasizes the importance of behavior in securing the respect and support of others. Because this warrior society so highly values its heroic code, it highly esteems those who conform to the code's principles. Beowulf vaunts himself as a great warrior and backs up his words by defeating Grendel; he is thus celebrated and received as a hero. Unferth, on the other hand, proves an empty chatterer, unwilling to fight Grendel or Grendel's mother. Though such verbal elements as boasts and stories are crucial to the warrior culture, heroes are, above all, defined by action.

QUOTATIONS

3.   Wise sir, do not grieve. It is always better
to avenge dear ones than to indulge in mourning.
For every one of us, living in this world
means waiting for our end. Let whoever can
win glory before death. When a warrior is gone,
that will be his best and only bulwark.

(1384–1389)

Beowulf utters this compressed statement of the heroic code after Grendel's mother kills Aeschere, Hrothgar's trusted advisor. Although Hrothgar's grief seems understandable in light of the principle of loyalty that operates in this culture, Beowulf speaks of it as an "indulgence"—an inappropriate and ineffective way of responding to the death of a comrade. Beowulf's reminder to Hrothgar that vengeance is the *real* warrior's response and the truest sign of love and loyalty reflects a fundamental value of warrior culture, namely an aggressive approach to life. Part of this approach involves the understanding that only reputation will perpetuate a warrior's existence after death. Beowulf, for example, perceives life as a race to glory ("Let whoever can / win glory before death"). This speech encapsulates the poem's tension between doom and death, on the one hand, and the necessity of behaving courageously and honorably, on the other. Beowulf's energetic emphasis on action helps temper the pessimism surrounding the inevitability of death that saturates the poem.

4.   Beowulf got ready,
donned his war-gear, indifferent to death;
his mighty, hand-forged, fine-webbed mail
would soon meet with the menace underwater.
It would keep the bone-cage of his body safe:
. . .
[His helmet] was of beaten gold,
princely headgear hooped and hasped
by a weapon-smith who had worked wonders. . . .

(1442–1452)

These lines describe Beowulf's preparation for his battle with Grendel's mother. The treatment of weaponry and armor is of great importance to the *Beowulf* poet. We see, here and elsewhere, that armor has a double history, much like a warrior does: a history of its making, which corresponds to the family lineage of an individual, and a history of performance, which corresponds to reputation. These lines seem to imply that the success of a weapon in battle is related to the skill with which it was crafted. The poet pays a great deal of attention, in general, to the craftsmanship that goes into physical objects and feats of language.

This passage is also characteristic in its exposition of the idea of fate. The poet's narration, though always in the past tense, often looks ahead to what will happen either in the immediate future—in the next few lines of the poem, even—or in the long term. The poet tells us, for example, that Beowulf's armor "would keep the bone-cage of his body safe." Though this tendency violates the reader's expectation that a narrator won't give away what will happen next, the poem is composed with a different set of literary expectations in mind. According to the warrior culture in which the poem is set, part of the meaning of fate is that future events are already contained in the present. To the *Beowulf* poet, then, it would seem foolish and pointless to try to counteract fate's powerful presence. Rather, he accepts it and includes it in his narrative.

5.   O flower of warriors, beware of that trap.
     Choose, dear Beowulf, the better part,
     eternal rewards. Do not give way to pride.
     For a brief while your strength is in bloom
     but it fades quickly; and soon there will follow
     illness or the sword to lay you low,
     or a sudden fire or surge of water
     or jabbing blade or javelin from the air
     or repellent age. Your piercing eye
     will dim and darken; and death will arrive,
     dear warrior, to sweep you away.

                                             (1758–1768)

This passage is the culmination of a long speech, often referred to as
"Hrothgar's sermon," in which Hrothgar warns Beowulf of the se-
ductive dangers of success after Beowulf defeats Grendel's mother.
Hrothgar asserts that power causes the soul to grow distracted by
fortune's favor and so to lose sight of future perils. The speech is
one of many points in the poem where the *Beowulf* poet overlays
Christian morals onto the pagan world that he depicts. The idea under consideration here is the Christian maxim "pride goeth before
a fall." Hrothgar specifically warns Beowulf not to "give way to
pride," an admonition that is discordant with the culture of boasts
and reputation that other parts of the poem celebrate. Hrothgar also
emphasizes to his young friend that life is fleeting and that he should
orient himself toward "eternal rewards"—a supremely Christian
idea—rather than worldly success. Throughout the poem, however,
it seems that eternal rewards can be won only *through* worldly success—the reward of fame for being a valiant warrior.

Hrothgar expresses the ephemeral quality of human life in beautiful terms. Calling Beowulf the "flower of warriors," he employs
an image that doesn't evoke Beowulf's strength and fortitude but
instead emphasizes the fragility of his life and the fact that his
youth—his "bloom"—will "fad[e] quickly." This choice of imagery
encapsulates the idea, implicit in this passage, that there are two
"death[s]" that threaten the warrior. He must be prepared not only
for a "jabbing blade or javelin from the air," which will wound
him, but also for "repellent age," which will eat away at his youthful audacity and force him to think in terms of honor, nobility, and
leadership that aren't dependent on mere physical prowess.

KEY FACTS

FULL TITLE
Beowulf

AUTHOR
Unknown

TYPE OF WORK
Poem

GENRE
Alliterative verse; elegy; resembles heroic epic, though smaller in scope than most classical epics

LANGUAGE
Anglo-Saxon (also called Old English)

TIME AND PLACE WRITTEN
Estimates of the date of composition range between 700 and 1000 A.D.; written in England

DATE OF FIRST PUBLICATION
The only manuscript in which *Beowulf* is preserved is thought to have been written around 1000 A.D.

PUBLISHER
The original poem exists only in manuscript form.

NARRATOR
A Christian narrator telling a story of pagan times

POINT OF VIEW
The narrator recounts the story in the third person, from a generally objective standpoint—detailing the action that occurs. The narrator does, however, have access to every character's depths. We see into the minds of most of the characters (even Grendel) at one point or another, and the narrative also moves forward and backward in time with considerable freedom.

TONE
The poet is generally enthusiastic about Beowulf's feats, but he often surrounds the events he narrates with a sense of doom.

TENSE
> Past, but with digressions into the distant past and predictions of the future

SETTING (TIME)
> The main action of the story is set around 500 A.D.; the narrative also recounts historical events that happened much earlier.

SETTING (PLACE)
> Denmark and Geatland (a region in what is now southern Sweden)

PROTAGONIST
> Beowulf

MAJOR CONFLICT
> The poem essentially consists of three parts. There are three central conflicts: Grendel's domination of Heorot Hall; the vengeance of Grendel's mother after Grendel is slain; and the rage of the dragon after a thief steals a treasure that it has been guarding. The poem's overarching conflict is between close-knit warrior societies and the various menaces that threaten their boundaries.

RISING ACTION
> Grendel's attack on Heorot, Beowulf's defeat of Grendel, and Grendel's mother's vengeful killing of Aeschere lead to the climactic encounter between Beowulf and Grendel's mother.

CLIMAX
> Beowulf's encounter with Grendel's mother constitutes the moment at which good and evil are in greatest tension.

FALLING ACTION
> Beowulf's glorious victory over Grendel's mother leads King Hrothgar to praise him as a worthy hero and to advise him about becoming king. It also helps Beowulf to transform from a brazen warrior into a reliable king.

THEMES
> The importance of establishing identity; tensions between the heroic code and other value systems; the difference between a good warrior and a good king

KEY FACTS

MOTIFS
Monsters; the oral tradition; the mead-hall

SYMBOLS
The golden torque; the banquet

FORESHADOWING
The funeral of Shield Sheafson, with which the poem opens, foreshadows Beowulf's funeral at the poem's end; the story of Sigemund told by the scop, or bard, foreshadows Beowulf's fight with the dragon; the story of King Heremod foreshadows Beowulf's eventual ascendancy to kingship.

STUDY QUESTIONS

1.   *How is* BEOWULF *structured? How does this structure relate to the theme or themes of the work as a whole?*

Beowulf is loosely divided into three parts, each of which centers around Beowulf's fight with a particular monster: first Grendel, then Grendel's mother, then the dragon. One can argue that this structure relates to the theme of the epic in that each monster presents a specific moral challenge against which the Anglo-Saxon heroic code can be measured and tested. Beowulf's fight with Grendel evokes the importance of reputation as a means of expanding one's existence beyond death. Grendel's great and terrifying nature ensures that Beowulf will long be celebrated for his heroic conquering of this foe. His subsequent encounter with Grendel's mother evokes the importance of vengeance. Just as Beowulf exacts revenge upon Grendel for killing Hrothgar's men, so too must Grendel's mother seek to purge her grief by slaying her son's murderer. Beowulf's final encounter with the dragon evokes a heroic approach to wyrd, or fate. Though he recognizes that his time has come and that he will thus not survive his clash with the dragon, he bravely embraces his duty to protect his people, sacrificing his life to save them.

Alternatively, one might make a division of the text into two parts, examining youth and old age as the two distinctive phases of Beowulf's life. Along these lines, the gap of fifty years between the first two conflicts and the last marks the dividing line. One of the main thematic points highlighted by such a division is the difference in responsibilities of the warrior and of the king. As a young warrior, Beowulf is free to travel afar to protect others, but as an old king, he must commit himself to guard his own people. Additionally, whereas Beowulf focuses on the heroic life early on, seeking to make a name for himself, he must focus on fate and the maintenance of his reputation late in life.

2. BEOWULF *is set in a male-dominated world full of violence and danger. What role does patriarchal history play in this world? Why does it matter to the warriors who their ancestors were?*

The obsession with patriarchal history manifests itself throughout *Beowulf,* which opens by tracing Hrothgar's male ancestry and constantly refers to characters as the sons of their fathers. An awareness of family lineage is one way in which the heroic code integrates itself into the warriors' most basic sense of identity. By placing such an emphasis on who their fathers were and how their fathers acted, the men of *Beowulf* bind themselves to a cycle of necessity governed by the heroic code. For example, because Beowulf's father owed a debt of loyalty to Hrothgar, Beowulf himself owes a debt of loyalty to Hrothgar. In this way, patriarchal history works to concretize and strengthen the warrior code in a world full of uncertainty and fear.

One might contrast this socially accepted version of patriarchal history with the various alternative models that the poem presents. Grendel, for example, descends from Cain, the biblical icon of familial disloyalty, and the avenging of his death is undertaken by a female relative rather than a male one. Examples of family discontinuity abound as well. For instance, Shield Sheafson is an orphan, and the Last Survivor represents the end of an entire race. Beowulf is similar to both of these characters—his father died while Beowulf was still young, and Beowulf himself dies without an heir. The anxiety about succession focuses attention on the ties between generations. Both Hrothgar and Hygelac depend on the loyalty of others if their sons are to inherit their respective kingships. All of these concerns help emphasize the importance of family heritage as a cultural value.

3.   *What role does religion play in* BEOWULF?

The *Beowulf* story has its roots in a pagan Saxon past, but by the time the epic was written down, almost all Anglo-Saxons had converted to Christianity. As a result, the *Beowulf* poet is at pains to resolve his Christian beliefs with the often quite un-Christian behavior of his characters. This tension leads to frequent asides about God, hell, and heaven—and to many allusions to the Old Testament throughout the work. In the end, however, the conflict proves simply irresolvable. Beowulf doesn't lead a particularly good life by Christian standards, but the poet cannot help but revere him. Though some of Beowulf's values—such as his dedication to his people and his willingness to dole out treasure—conceivably overlap with Christian values, he ultimately lives for the preservation of earthly glory after death, not for entrance into heaven. Though his death in the encounter with the dragon clearly proves his mortality (and perhaps moral fallibility), the poem itself stands as a testament to the raw greatness of his life, ensuring his ascension into the secular heaven of warrior legend.

STUDY QUESTIONS

How to Write
Literary Analysis

The Literary Essay: A Step-by-Step Guide

When you read for pleasure, your only goal is enjoyment. You might find yourself reading to get caught up in an exciting story, to learn about an interesting time or place, or just to pass time. Maybe you're looking for inspiration, guidance, or a reflection of your own life. There are as many different, valid ways of reading a book as there are books in the world.

When you read a work of literature in an English class, however, you're being asked to read in a special way: you're being asked to perform *literary analysis*. To analyze something means to break it down into smaller parts and then examine how those parts work, both individually and together. Literary analysis involves examining all the parts of a novel, play, short story, or poem—elements such as character, setting, tone, and imagery—and thinking about how the author uses those elements to create certain effects.

A literary essay isn't a book review: you're not being asked whether or not you liked a book or whether you'd recommend it to another reader. A literary essay also isn't like the kind of book report you wrote when you were younger, where your teacher wanted you to summarize the book's action. A high school- or college-level literary essay asks, "How does this piece of literature actually work?" "How does it do what it does?" and, "Why might the author have made the choices he or she did?"

The Seven Steps

No one is born knowing how to analyze literature; it's a skill you learn and a process you can master. As you gain more practice with this kind of thinking and writing, you'll be able to craft a method that works best for you. But until then, here are seven basic steps to writing a well-constructed literary essay:

1. *Ask questions*
2. *Collect evidence*
3. *Construct a thesis*

4. Develop and organize arguments
5. Write the introduction
6. Write the body paragraphs
7. Write the conclusion

1. ASK QUESTIONS

When you're assigned a literary essay in class, your teacher will often provide you with a list of writing prompts. Lucky you! Now all you have to do is choose one. Do yourself a favor and pick a topic that interests you. You'll have a much better (not to mention easier) time if you start off with something you enjoy thinking about. If you are asked to come up with a topic by yourself, though, you might start to feel a little panicked. Maybe you have too many ideas—or none at all. Don't worry. Take a deep breath and start by asking yourself these questions:

- **What struck you?** Did a particular image, line, or scene linger in your mind for a long time? If it fascinated you, chances are you can draw on it to write a fascinating essay.

- **What confused you?** Maybe you were surprised to see a character act in a certain way, or maybe you didn't understand why the book ended the way it did. Confusing moments in a work of literature are like a loose thread in a sweater: if you pull on it, you can unravel the entire thing. Ask yourself why the author chose to write about that character or scene the way he or she did and you might tap into some important insights about the work as a whole.

- **Did you notice any patterns?** Is there a phrase that the main character uses constantly or an image that repeats throughout the book? If you can figure out how that pattern weaves through the work and what the significance of that pattern is, you've almost got your entire essay mapped out.

- **Did you notice any contradictions or ironies?** Great works of literature are complex; great literary essays recognize and explain those complexities. Maybe the title (*Happy Days*) totally disagrees with the book's subject matter (hungry orphans dying in the woods). Maybe the main character acts one way around his family and a completely different way around his friends and associates. If you can find a way to explain a work's contradictory elements, you've got the seeds of a great essay.

At this point, you don't need to know exactly what you're going to say about your topic; you just need a place to begin your exploration. You can help direct your reading and brainstorming by formulating your topic as a *question*, which you'll then try to answer in your essay. The best questions invite critical debates and discussions, not just a rehashing of the summary. Remember, you're looking for something you can *prove or argue* based on evidence you find in the text. Finally, remember to keep the scope of your question in mind: is this a topic you can adequately address within the word or page limit you've been given? Conversely, is this a topic big enough to fill the required length?

Good Questions
"Are Romeo and Juliet's parents responsible for the deaths of their children?"

"Why do pigs keep showing up in Lord of the Flies?*"*

"Are Dr. Frankenstein and his monster alike? How?"

Bad Questions
"What happens to Scout in To Kill a Mockingbird?*"*

"What do the other characters in Julius Caesar *think about Caesar?"*

"How does Hester Prynne in The Scarlet Letter *remind me of my sister?"*

---

2. Collect Evidence
Once you know what question you want to answer, it's time to scour the book for things that will help you answer the question. Don't worry if you don't know what you want to say yet—right now you're just collecting ideas and material and letting it all percolate. Keep track of passages, symbols, images, or scenes that deal with your topic. Eventually, you'll start making connections between these examples and your thesis will emerge.

Here's a brief summary of the various parts that compose each and every work of literature. These are the elements that you will analyze in your essay, and which you will offer as evidence to support your arguments. For more on the parts of literary works, see the Glossary of Literary Terms at the end of this section.

LITERARY ANALYSIS

Elements of Story   These are the *what*s of the work—what happens, where it happens, and to whom it happens.

- **Plot:** All of the events and actions of the work.
- **Character:** The people who act and are acted upon in a literary work. The main character of a work is known as the *protagonist.*
- **Conflict:** The central tension in the work. In most cases, the protagonist wants something, while opposing forces (antagonists) hinder the protagonist's progress.
- **Setting:** When and where the work takes place. Elements of setting include location, time period, time of day, weather, social atmosphere, and economic conditions.
- **Narrator:** The person telling the story. The narrator may straightforwardly report what happens, convey the subjective opinions and perceptions of one or more characters, or provide commentary and opinion in his or her own voice.
- **Themes:** The main idea or message of the work—usually an abstract idea about people, society, or life in general. A work may have many themes, which may be in tension with one another.

Elements of Style   These are the *how*s—how the characters speak, how the story is constructed, and how language is used throughout the work.

- **Structure and organization:** How the parts of the work are assembled. Some novels are narrated in a linear, chronological fashion, while others skip around in time. Some plays follow a traditional three- or five-act structure, while others are a series of loosely connected scenes. Some authors deliberately leave gaps in their works, leaving readers to puzzle out the missing information. A work's structure and organization can tell you a lot about the kind of message it wants to convey.
- **Point of view:** The perspective from which a story is told. In *first-person point of view,* the narrator involves him or herself in the story. ("I went to the store"; "We watched in horror as the bird slammed into the window.") A first-person narrator is usually the protagonist of the work, but not always. In *third-person point of view,* the narrator does not participate

in the story. A third-person narrator may closely follow a specific character, recounting that individual character's thoughts or experiences, or it may be what we call an *omniscient* narrator. Omniscient narrators see and know all: they can witness any event in any time or place and are privy to the inner thoughts and feelings of all characters. Remember that the narrator and the author are not the same thing!

- **Diction:** Word choice. Whether a character uses dry, clinical language or flowery prose with lots of exclamation points can tell you a lot about his or her attitude and personality.

- **Syntax:** Word order and sentence construction. Syntax is a crucial part of establishing an author's narrative voice. Ernest Hemingway, for example, is known for writing in very short, straightforward sentences, while James Joyce characteristically wrote in long, incredibly complicated lines.

- **Tone:** The mood or feeling of the text. Diction and syntax often contribute to the tone of a work. A novel written in short, clipped sentences that use small, simple words might feel brusque, cold, or matter-of-fact.

- **Imagery:** Language that appeals to the senses, representing things that can be seen, smelled, heard, tasted, or touched.

- **Figurative language:** Language that is not meant to be interpreted literally. The most common types of figurative language are *metaphors* and *similes*, which compare two unlike things in order to suggest a similarity between them— for example, "All the world's a stage," or "The moon is like a ball of green cheese." (Metaphors say one thing *is* another thing; similes claim that one thing is *like* another thing.)

---

3. CONSTRUCT A THESIS

When you've examined all the evidence you've collected and know how you want to answer the question, it's time to write your thesis statement. A *thesis* is a claim about a work of literature that needs to be supported by evidence and arguments. The thesis statement is the heart of the literary essay, and the bulk of your paper will be spent trying to prove this claim. A good thesis will be:

- **Arguable.** "*The Great Gatsby* describes New York society in the 1920s" isn't a thesis—it's a fact.

- **Provable through textual evidence.** "*Hamlet* is a confusing but ultimately very well-written play" is a weak thesis because it offers the writer's personal opinion about the book. Yes, it's arguable, but it's not a claim that can be proved or supported with examples taken from the play itself.

- **Surprising.** "Both George and Lenny change a great deal in *Of Mice and Men*" is a weak thesis because it's obvious. A really strong thesis will argue for a reading of the text that is not immediately apparent.

- **Specific.** "Dr. Frankenstein's monster tells us a lot about the human condition" is *almost* a really great thesis statement, but it's still too vague. What does the writer mean by "a lot"? *How* does the monster tell us so much about the human condition?

GOOD THESIS STATEMENTS

Question: In *Romeo and Juliet*, which is more powerful in shaping the lovers' story: fate or foolishness?

Thesis: "Though Shakespeare defines Romeo and Juliet as 'star-crossed lovers' and images of stars and planets appear throughout the play, a closer examination of that celestial imagery reveals that the stars are merely witnesses to the characters' foolish activities and not the causes themselves."

Question: How does the bell jar function as a symbol in Sylvia Plath's *The Bell Jar*?

Thesis: "A bell jar is a bell-shaped glass that has three basic uses: to hold a specimen for observation, to contain gases, and to maintain a vacuum. The bell jar appears in each of these capacities in *The Bell Jar*, Plath's semi-autobiographical novel, and each appearance marks a different stage in Esther's mental breakdown."

Question: Would Piggy in *The Lord of the Flies* make a good island leader if he were given the chance?

Thesis: "Though the intelligent, rational, and innovative Piggy has the mental characteristics of a good leader, he ultimately lacks the social skills necessary to be an effective one. Golding emphasizes this point by giving Piggy a foil in the charismatic Jack, whose magnetic personality allows him to capture and wield power effectively, if not always wisely."

4. DEVELOP AND ORGANIZE ARGUMENTS

The reasons and examples that support your thesis will form the middle paragraphs of your essay. Since you can't really write your thesis statement until you know how you'll structure your argument, you'll probably end up working on steps 3 and 4 at the same time.

There's no single method of argumentation that will work in every context. One essay prompt might ask you to compare and contrast two characters, while another asks you to trace an image through a given work of literature. These questions require different kinds of answers and therefore different kinds of arguments. Below, we'll discuss three common kinds of essay prompts and some strategies for constructing a solid, well-argued case.

TYPES OF LITERARY ESSAYS

- **Compare and contrast**

  Compare and contrast the characters of Huck and Jim in THE ADVENTURES OF HUCKLEBERRY FINN.

  Chances are you've written this kind of essay before. In an academic literary context, you'll organize your arguments the same way you would in any other class. You can either go *subject by subject* or *point by point*. In the former, you'll discuss one character first and then the second. In the latter, you'll choose several traits (attitude toward life, social status, images and metaphors associated with the character) and devote a paragraph to each. You may want to use a mix of these two approaches—for example, you may want to spend a paragraph a piece broadly sketching Huck's and Jim's personalities before transitioning into a paragraph or two that describes a few key points of comparison. This can be a highly effective strategy if you want to make a counterintuitive argument—that, despite seeming to be totally different, the two objects being compared are actually similar in a very important way (or vice versa). Remember that your essay should reveal something fresh or unexpected about the text, so think beyond the obvious parallels and differences.

- **Trace**

  Choose an image—for example, birds, knives, or eyes—and trace that image throughout MACBETH.

  Sounds pretty easy, right? All you need to do is read the play, underline every appearance of a knife in *Macbeth*, and then list them in your essay in the order they appear, right? Well, not exactly. Your teacher doesn't want a simple catalog of examples. He or she wants to see you make *connections* between those examples—that's the difference between summarizing and analyzing. In the *Macbeth* example above, think about the different contexts in which knives appear in the play and to what effect. In *Macbeth,* there are real knives and imagined knives; knives that kill and knives that simply threaten. Categorize and classify your examples to give them some order. Finally, always keep the overall effect in mind. After you choose and analyze your examples, you should come to some greater understanding about the work, as well as your chosen image, symbol, or phrase's role in developing the major themes and stylistic strategies of that work.

* **Debate**

  Is the society depicted in 1984 good for its citizens?

  In this kind of essay, you're being asked to debate a moral, ethical, or aesthetic issue regarding the work. You might be asked to judge a character or group of characters (*Is Caesar responsible for his own demise?*) or the work itself (*Is* JANE EYRE *a feminist novel?*). For this kind of essay, there are two important points to keep in mind. First, don't simply base your arguments on your personal feelings and reactions. Every literary essay expects you to read and analyze the work, so search for evidence in the text. What do characters in *1984* have to say about the government of Oceania? What images does Orwell use that might give you a hint about his attitude toward the government? As in any debate, you also need to make sure that you define all the necessary terms before you begin to argue your case. What does it mean to be a "good" society? What makes a novel "feminist"? You should define your terms right up front, in the first paragraph after your introduction.

  Second, remember that strong literary essays make contrary and surprising arguments. Try to think outside the box. In the *1984* example above, it seems like the obvious answer would be no, the totalitarian society depicted in Orwell's novel is *not* good for its citizens. But can you think of any arguments for the opposite side? Even if your final assertion is that the novel depicts a cruel, repressive, and therefore harmful society, acknowledging and responding to the counterargument will strengthen your overall case.

5. WRITE THE INTRODUCTION

Your introduction sets up the entire essay. It's where you present your topic and articulate the particular issues and questions you'll be addressing. It's also where you, as the writer, introduce yourself to your readers. A persuasive literary essay immediately establishes its writer as a knowledgeable, authoritative figure.

An introduction can vary in length depending on the overall length of the essay, but in a traditional five-paragraph essay it should be no longer than one paragraph. However long it is, your introduction needs to:

- **Provide any necessary context.** Your introduction should situate the reader and let him or her know what to expect. What book are you discussing? Which characters? What topic will you be addressing?

- **Answer the "So what?" question.** Why is this topic important, and why is your particular position on the topic noteworthy? Ideally, your introduction should pique the reader's interest by suggesting how your argument is surprising or otherwise counterintuitive. Literary essays make unexpected connections and reveal less-than-obvious truths.

- **Present your thesis.** This usually happens at or very near the end of your introduction.

- **Indicate the shape of the essay to come.** Your reader should finish reading your introduction with a good sense of the scope of your essay as well as the path you'll take toward proving your thesis. You don't need to spell out every step, but you do need to suggest the organizational pattern you'll be using.

Your introduction should not:

- **Be vague.** Beware of the two killer words in literary analysis: *interesting* and *important*. Of course the work, question, or example is interesting and important—that's why you're writing about it!

- **Open with any grandiose assertions.** Many student readers think that beginning their essays with a flamboyant statement such as, "Since the dawn of time, writers have been fascinated with the topic of free will," makes them sound important and commanding. You know what? It actually sounds pretty amateurish.

- **Wildly praise the work.** Another typical mistake student writers make is extolling the work or author. Your teacher doesn't need to be told that "Shakespeare is perhaps the greatest writer in the English language." You can mention a work's reputation in passing—by referring to *The Adventures of Huckleberry Finn* as "Mark Twain's enduring classic," for example—but don't make a point of bringing it up unless that reputation is key to your argument.

- **Go off-topic.** Keep your introduction streamlined and to the point. Don't feel the need to throw in all kinds of bells and whistles in order to impress your reader—just get to the point as quickly as you can, without skimping on any of the required steps.

---

6. WRITE THE BODY PARAGRAPHS

Once you've written your introduction, you'll take the arguments you developed in step 4 and turn them into your body paragraphs. The organization of this middle section of your essay will largely be determined by the argumentative strategy you use, but no matter how you arrange your thoughts, your body paragraphs need to do the following:

- **Begin with a strong topic sentence.** Topic sentences are like signs on a highway: they tell the reader where they are and where they're going. A good topic sentence not only alerts readers to what issue will be discussed in the following paragraph but also gives them a sense of what argument will be made *about* that issue. "Rumor and gossip play an important role in *The Crucible*" isn't a strong topic sentence because it doesn't tell us very much. "The community's constant gossiping creates an environment that allows false accusations to flourish" is a much stronger topic sentence— it not only tells us *what* the paragraph will discuss (gossip) but *how* the paragraph will discuss the topic (by showing how gossip creates a set of conditions that leads to the play's climactic action).

- **Fully and completely develop a single thought.** Don't skip around in your paragraph or try to stuff in too much material. Body paragraphs are like bricks: each individual

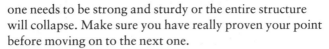

one needs to be strong and sturdy or the entire structure will collapse. Make sure you have really proven your point before moving on to the next one.

- **Use transitions effectively.** Good literary essay writers know that each paragraph must be clearly and strongly linked to the material around it. Think of each paragraph as a response to the one that precedes it. Use transition words and phrases such as *however, similarly, on the contrary, therefore,* and *furthermore* to indicate what kind of response you're making.

---

7. WRITE THE CONCLUSION
Just as you used the introduction to ground your readers in the topic before providing your thesis, you'll use the conclusion to quickly summarize the specifics learned thus far and then hint at the broader implications of your topic. A good conclusion will:

- **Do more than simply restate the thesis.** If your thesis argued that *The Catcher in the Rye* can be read as a Christian allegory, don't simply end your essay by saying, "And that is why *The Catcher in the Rye* can be read as a Christian allegory." If you've constructed your arguments well, this kind of statement will just be redundant.

- **Synthesize the arguments, not summarize them.** Similarly, don't repeat the details of your body paragraphs in your conclusion. The reader has already read your essay, and chances are it's not so long that they've forgotten all your points by now.

- **Revisit the "So what?" question.** In your introduction, you made a case for why your topic and position are important. You should close your essay with the same sort of gesture. What do your readers know now that they didn't know before? How will that knowledge help them better appreciate or understand the work overall?

- **Move from the specific to the general.** Your essay has most likely treated a very specific element of the work—a single character, a small set of images, or a particular passage. In your conclusion, try to show how this narrow discussion has wider implications for the work overall. If your essay on *To Kill a Mockingbird* focused on the character of Boo Radley, for example, you might want to include a bit in your conclusion about how he fits into the novel's larger message about childhood, innocence, or family life.

- **Stay relevant.** Your conclusion should suggest new directions of thought, but it shouldn't be treated as an opportunity to pad your essay with all the extra, interesting ideas you came up with during your brainstorming sessions but couldn't fit into the essay proper. Don't attempt to stuff in unrelated queries or too many abstract thoughts.

- **Avoid making overblown closing statements.** A conclusion should open up your highly specific, focused discussion, but it should do so without drawing a sweeping lesson about life or human nature. Making such observations may be part of the point of reading, but it's almost always a mistake in essays, where these observations tend to sound overly dramatic or simply silly.

A+ Essay Checklist

Congratulations! If you've followed all the steps we've outlined above, you should have a solid literary essay to show for all your efforts. What if you've got your sights set on an A+? To write the kind of superlative essay that will be rewarded with a perfect grade, keep the following rubric in mind. These are the qualities that teachers expect to see in a truly A+ essay. How does yours stack up?

- ✓ Demonstrates a thorough understanding of the book
- ✓ Presents an original, compelling argument
- ✓ Thoughtfully analyzes the text's formal elements
- ✓ Uses appropriate and insightful examples
- ✓ Structures ideas in a logical and progressive order
- ✓ Demonstrates a mastery of sentence construction, transitions, grammar, spelling, and word choice

Suggested Essay Topics

1. *What role does the mead-hall play in Anglo-Saxon warrior culture? What is the proper relationship between a lord and his warriors? What examples can you find throughout* BEOWULF?

2. *What is the role of women in the heroic culture of* BEOWULF?

3. *What role do the digressions play in* BEOWULF? *What light do they shed on the main action?*

4. *Is Beowulf an ideal hero and king? Is there anything lacking in his character?*

5. *Would you say that the characters in* BEOWULF *are as psychologically complex those in modern works of literature? Do they undergo any development as the poem progresses?*

A+ Student Essay

What is the role of treasure in *Beowulf*?

In our culture, preoccupation with material goods usually connotes shallowness, and the pursuit of riches is often seen as incompatible—or at least difficult to reconcile—with our moral convictions. In *Beowulf*, however, the Danes, Geats, and Swedes' collective reverence for treasure is not represented as a shortcoming or moral weakness. In fact, the poem often uses treasure as a symbol of the Scandinavian people's most cherished cultural values.

In *Beowulf*, kings, heroes, and other powerful men must continuously establish their reputations, both those they have inherited and those they have earned. Characters accomplish the former by reminding listeners of their famous ancestors and the latter by collecting treasures. The magnificent rewards Beowulf receives from Hrothgar testify to the Geatish warrior's valor and prowess, just as the majestic Heorot signifies Hrothgar's power. Sometimes, a splendid object is enough to gain a man respect, even without his having earned it through brave deeds—the Danish guard who watches Beowulf's ship, for example, gets a sword "with gold fittings" that in the future will make him "a respected man / at his place on the mead-bench" (1901–1903). On the other hand, loss of treasure symbolizes a fall from power. After Beowulf dies, the poet announces the end of a glorious Geatish era by noting that "no follower" will wear the treasure Beowulf wins from the dragon in his memory, "nor lovely woman / link and attach [it] as a torque around her neck." Treasure symbolizes prosperity and stability; without these attributes, the Geatish clan can no longer be seen in jewels and finery.

The kings of *Beowulf* also use treasure to solidify their most important bonds: those with their followers, and those with other nations. Each king has a duty to give his most loyal thanes riches, a responsibility indicated by the frequent use of royal epithets such as "ring-giver," "gift-lord," and "gold-friend to retainers." The act is not only a matter of custom, but also of honor. Among his other crimes, the wicked Heremod is accused of giving "no more rings / to honor the Danes" (1719–1720). In this culture, treasure is not for hoarding but for circulating in socially useful ways. On an international level, the kings use treasure to strengthen alliances and avoid conflict among the various Scandinavian tribes. Friendly tribes may exchange gifts, while hostile nations may pacify one another with gold or with the paying of blood tributes. In this scheme, women represent the most valuable token of exchange, as kings often betroth their daughters to foreign rulers for political gain. The constant mention of the gold and jewels that adorn Wealtheow suggest her political value: The queen not only *wears* treasure, in a sense, she *is* treasure.

Finally, treasure also symbolizes the contradictory feelings the Geats and Danes have toward death, a constant presence in this dark, brutal era. Though the poet writes from an explicitly Christian perspective, the Geats and Danes seem to lack a notion of a divine afterlife. In this world, human existence remains limited to the mortal lifespan. However, people have the opportunity to achieve some kind of afterlife by accruing wealth, prestige, and glory while they live: Owning significant treasure increases the likelihood that one's name and reputation will live on after death. At the same time, the Geats and Danes realize that treasure remains earthbound, unable to accompany its owner into the hereafter. Both of these notions figure into the Scandinavian funeral ritual of sending a king off to sea in a burning ship filled with treasure. The more rings, swords, and coats of mail piled upon the ship, the greater the king's glory; however, those riches eventually burn away or become otherwise lost to the king's people. In *Beowulf,* treasure simultaneously has an eternal and an evanescent quality.

Amidst the general veneration of treasure, though, come some discordant notes. In one of the poem's most mournful moments, the narrator describes "some forgotten person" burying the collective riches of his entire, equally forgotten race. In this case, the accumulation of glorious wealth was not enough to gain a lasting legacy, and the treasure only enhances the survivor's terrible loneliness, as he is "left with nobody / to bear a sword or to burnish plated goblets / put a sheen on the cup" (2252–2253). Just a few lines earlier, Beowulf had imagined how the sight of the Danes wearing "glittering regalia" and "burnished ring-mail" originally belonging to the Heatho-Bards would provoke the Heatho-Bards to viciously attack their guests. And after Beowulf's death, the poet bitterly describes how the treasure left in the dragon's lair is "as useless to men now as it ever was" (3168). As the poem looks ahead to both the Danish war with the Heatho-Bards and the Geatish devastation following Beowulf's death, the creeping disillusion with wealth hints at the darkness looming on the horizon.

LITERARY ANALYSIS

GLOSSARY OF LITERARY TERMS

ANTAGONIST

The entity that acts to frustrate the goals of the *protagonist*. The antagonist is usually another *character* but may also be a non-human force.

ANTIHERO / ANTIHEROINE

A *protagonist* who is not admirable or who challenges notions of what should be considered admirable.

CHARACTER

A person, animal, or any other thing with a personality that appears in a *narrative*.

CLIMAX

The moment of greatest intensity in a text or the major turning point in the *plot*.

CONFLICT

The central struggle that moves the *plot* forward. The conflict can be the *protagonist*'s struggle against fate, nature, society, or another person.

FIRST-PERSON POINT OF VIEW

A literary style in which the *narrator* tells the story from his or her own *point of view* and refers to himself or herself as "I." The narrator may be an active participant in the story or just an observer.

HERO / HEROINE

The principal *character* in a literary work or *narrative*.

IMAGERY

Language that brings to mind sense-impressions, representing things that can be seen, smelled, heard, tasted, or touched.

MOTIF

A recurring idea, structure, contrast, or device that develops or informs the major *themes* of a work of literature.

NARRATIVE

A story.

NARRATOR

The person (sometimes a *character*) who tells a story; the *voice* assumed by the writer. The narrator and the author of the work of literature are not the same person.

PLOT

The arrangement of the events in a story, including the sequence in which they are told, the relative emphasis they are given, and the causal connections between events.

POINT OF VIEW

The *perspective* that a *narrative* takes toward the events it describes.

PROTAGONIST

The main *character* around whom the story revolves.

SETTING

The location of a *narrative* in time and space. Setting creates mood or atmosphere.

SUBPLOT

A secondary *plot* that is of less importance to the overall story but may serve as a point of contrast or comparison to the main plot.

SYMBOL

An object, *character*, figure, or color that is used to represent an abstract idea or concept. Unlike an *emblem*, a symbol may have different meanings in different contexts.

SYNTAX

The way the words in a piece of writing are put together to form lines, phrases, or clauses; the basic structure of a piece of writing.

THEME

A fundamental and universal idea explored in a literary work.

TONE

The author's attitude toward the subject or *characters* of a story or poem or toward the reader.

VOICE

An author's individual way of using language to reflect his or her own personality and attitudes. An author communicates voice through *tone*, *diction*, and *syntax*.

A NOTE ON PLAGIARISM

Plagiarism—presenting someone else's work as your own—rears its ugly head in many forms. Many students know that copying text without citing it is unacceptable. But some don't realize that even if you're not quoting directly, but instead are paraphrasing or summarizing, *it is plagiarism* unless you cite the source.

Here are the most common forms of plagiarism:

- Using an author's phrases, sentences, or paragraphs without citing the source
- Paraphrasing an author's ideas without citing the source
- Passing off another student's work as your own

How do you steer clear of plagiarism? You should *always* acknowledge all words and ideas that aren't your own by using quotation marks around verbatim text or citations like footnotes and endnotes to note another writer's ideas. For more information on how to give credit when credit is due, ask your teacher for guidance or visit www.sparknotes.com.

REVIEW & RESOURCES

QUIZ

1. Who is the father of Shield Sheafson?

   A. Beowulf
   B. Hrothgar
   C. Grendel
   D. Sheafson is an orphan.

2. How does Hrothgar know of Beowulf?

   A. Beowulf once proposed to his daughter.
   B. Hrothgar was friends with Beowulf's father.
   C. Beowulf had gained a widespread reputation after slaying a dragon.
   D. He read about him on the Internet.

3. About how long is the dragon?

   A. 50 feet
   B. 20 feet
   C. 100 feet
   D. 200 feet

4. How long does Beowulf reign as king of the Geats?

   A. 30 years
   B. 40 years
   C. 50 years
   D. 60 years

5. What, according to Beowulf, is better than mourning a death?

   A. Celebrating a birth
   B. Avenging a death
   C. Drinking one's sorrows away
   D. Making peace with one's enemies

6. Who helps Beowulf against the dragon?

   A. Wulfgar
   B. Unferth
   C. Hrothgar
   D. Wiglaf

7. Who taunts Beowulf in Heorot?

   A. Unferth
   B. Hrothgar
   C. Wiglaf
   D. Wealhtheow

8. Who is Modthryth?

   A. A Danish thane
   B. King of the Swedes
   C. A wicked queen of legend
   D. A dragon

9. From whom is Grendel descended?

   A. Satan
   B. Cain
   C. Judas
   D. Ecgtheow

10. Who is queen of the Geats?

    A. Wealhtheow
    B. Modthryth
    C. Unferth
    D. Hygd

11. Whom does Grendel's mother abduct and decapitate?

    A. Aeschere
    B. Wulfgar
    C. Hrothgar
    D. Beowulf

12. How many Geats does Grendel kill?

    A. Eleven
    B. Eight
    C. One
    D. Four

13. What is Hrunting?

    A. A mead-hall
    B. A sword
    C. A lake
    D. A helmet

14. Where do the Geats place Beowulf's Barrow?

    A. In Grendel's swamp
    B. In the dragon's lair
    C. In the palace temple
    D. On a cliff overlooking the sea

15. Who is Beowulf's father?

    A. Ecgtheow
    B. Hrothgar
    C. Wulfgar
    D. Wealhtheow

16. What is wyrd?

    A. The Anglo-Saxon concept of "word," as in word of honor
    B. The Anglo-Saxon term for "worm," as in dragon
    C. The Anglo-Saxon concept of "fate"
    D. The Anglo-Saxon word that expresses the culture's valuing of oratorical skill

17. Where do Grendel and his mother live?

    A. In a palace
    B. In a mead-hall
    C. In a barrow
    D. In a lake

18. What is a scop?

    A. A mead-hall
    B. A poet
    C. A god
    D. A ship

19. Who guides Beowulf to the dragon's barrow?

    A. Wulfgar
    B. The thief
    C. The slave-girl
    D. Hygd

20. Who gives Hygd three horses?

    A. Hygelac
    B. Hrothgar
    C. Beowulf
    D. Finn

21. Which character is descended from Shield Sheafson?

    A. Beowulf
    B. Wiglaf
    C. Ecgtheow
    D. Hrothgar

22. What is the name of Hrothgar's wife?

    A. Wealhtheow
    B. Hygd
    C. Modthryth
    D. Grendel

23. How did the dragon's treasure get in the barrow?

    A. The dragon hauled it there with his teeth.
    B. Hygelac had it buried there after he died.
    C. The boat containing the body of Shield Sheafson landed there.
    D. It was buried there by the last survivor of a forgotten race.

24. What is Hygelac wearing when he dies?

    A.   His grandfather's armor
    B.   Wealhtheow's torque
    C.   An invisibility suit
    D.   A tutu

25. From about when does the only existing *Beowulf* manuscript date?

    A.   700 A.D.
    B.   1000 A.D.
    C.   700 B.C.
    D.   50 A.D.

SUGGESTIONS FOR FURTHER READING

BAKER, PETER S. *The* BEOWULF *Reader: Basic Readings.* New York: Garland Publishing, 2000.

BJORK, ROBERT E., and JOHN D. NILES. *A* BEOWULF *Handbook.* Lincoln, NE: University of Nebraska Press, reprint edition 2007.

BLOOM, HAROLD, ed. BEOWULF: *Modern Critical Interpretations.* New York: Chelsea House, 1987.

CHAMBERS, R. W. BEOWULF: *An Introduction to the Study of the Poem.* Cambridge, UK: Cambridge University Press, 1959.

FRY, DONALD K., ed. *The* BEOWULF *Poet: A Collection of Critical Essays.* Englewood Cliffs, NJ: Prentice-Hall, 1968.

GRIGSBY, JOHN. *Beowulf and Grendel: The Truth Behind England's Oldest Legend.* London: Duncan Baird Publishers, 2006.

IRVING, EDWARD B., JR. *Introduction to* BEOWULF. Englewood Cliffs, NJ: Prentice-Hall, 1969.

NILES, JOHN D. BEOWULF: *The Poem and Its Tradition.* Cambridge, MA: Harvard University Press, 1983.

PEARSALL, DEREK. *Old English and Middle English Poetry.* London: Routledge, 1977.

SparkNotes Literature Guides

1984
The Adventures of
  Huckleberry Finn
The Adventures of
  Tom Sawyer
The Aeneid
All Quiet on the
  Western Front
And Then There Were
  None
Angela's Ashes
Animal Farm
Anna Karenina
Anne of Green Gables
Anthem
As I Lay Dying
The Awakening
The Bean Trees
Beloved
Beowulf
Billy Budd
Black Boy
Bless Me, Ultima
The Bluest Eye
Brave New World
The Brothers
  Karamazov
The Call of the Wild
Candide
The Canterbury Tales
Catch-22
The Catcher in the Rye
The Chocolate War
The Chosen
Cold Sassy Tree
The Color Purple
The Count of Monte
  Cristo
Crime and Punishment
The Crucible
Cry, the Beloved
  Country
Cyrano de Bergerac
David Copperfield
Death of a Salesman
Death of Socrates
Diary of a Young Girl

A Doll's House
Don Quixote
Dr. Faustus
Dr. Jekyll and Mr. Hyde
Dracula
Edith Hamilton's
  Mythology
Emma
Ethan Frome
Fahrenheit 451
A Farewell to Arms
The Fellowship of the
  Rings
Flowers for Algernon
For Whom the Bell
  Tolls
The Fountainhead
Frankenstein
The Giver
The Glass Menagerie
The Good Earth
The Grapes of Wrath
Great Expectations
The Great Gatsby
Grendel
Gulliver's Travels
Hamlet
The Handmaid's Tale
Hard Times
Heart of Darkness
Henry IV, Part I
Henry V
Hiroshima
The Hobbit
The House on Mango
  Street
I Know Why the Caged
  Bird Sings
The Iliad
The Importance of
  Being Earnest
Inferno
Invisible Man
Jane Eyre
Johnny Tremain
The Joy Luck Club
Julius Caesar

The Jungle
The Killer Angels
King Lear
The Last of the
  Mohicans
Les Misérables
A Lesson Before Dying
Little Women
Lord of the Flies
Macbeth
Madame Bovary
The Merchant of
  Venice
A Midsummer Night's
  Dream
Moby-Dick
Much Ado About
  Nothing
My Ántonia
Narrative of the Life of
  Frederick Douglass
Native Son
The New Testament
Night
The Odyssey
Oedipus Plays
Of Mice and Men
The Old Man and
  the Sea
The Old Testament
Oliver Twist
The Once and Future
  King
One Flew Over the
  Cuckoo's Nest
One Hundred Years of
  Solitude
Othello
Our Town
The Outsiders
Paradise Lost
The Pearl
The Picture of Dorian
  Gray
Poe's Short Stories
A Portrait of the Artist
  as a Young Man

Pride and Prejudice
The Prince
A Raisin in the Sun
The Red Badge of
  Courage
The Republic
The Return of the King
Richard III
Robinson Crusoe
Romeo and Juliet
Scarlet Letter
A Separate Peace
Silas Marner
Sir Gawain and the
  Green Knight
Slaughterhouse-Five
Song of Solomon
The Sound and the
  Fury
The Stranger
A Streetcar Named
  Desire
The Sun Also Rises
A Tale of Two Cities
The Taming of the
  Shrew
The Tempest
Tess of the
  d'Urbervilles
The Things They
  Carried
The Two Towers
Their Eyes Were
  Watching God
Things Fall Apart
To Kill a Mockingbird
Treasure Island
Twelfth Night
Ulysses
Uncle Tom's Cabin
Walden
War and Peace
Wuthering Heights
A Yellow Raft in Blue
  Water

Visit sparknotes.com for many more!